HEROES OF THE BIBLE

JOSEPH
and his BROTHERS

by
Claudia Vurnakes

Published by Playmore Inc., Publishers
and Waldman Publishing Corp.,
New York, New York

HEROES OF THE BIBLE

Series Editor
Claudia Vurnakes

This book is written to help young readers
understand and appreciate the stories of the Bible.
It is based on traditional and contemporary translations.
It is not intended to replace regular reading
and study of the Bible.

CONTENTS

Joseph finds his brothers.

CHAPTER 1
The Blessing of Sons

Reuben, Levi, Issachar and the others—where were they? Where could they be?

Seventeen-year-old Joseph searched the horizon. The brilliant sunset was quickly fading to black, and his older brothers and their flocks were nowhere in sight. They had all agreed to meet here for the night. Something must have happened to keep them, Joseph thought. What if a lion had attacked, or they had surprised a bear in its den? What if falling rocks had blocked their way? Joseph kept straining to see. Maybe his brothers were lying somewhere, hurt and helpless. What should he do? What could he do? Where were they? Worries buzzed like flies in the young man's head.

A familiar sound caught his attention.

Impatient bleating snapped Joseph to attention. He looked down at the sheep milling around his feet. Poor thirsty creatures! No matter what had happened to his brothers, he still had to care for his flocks and settle them for the night. Joseph led the way up the trail to a spring that bubbled out of the rocky hillside. Ewes and lambs rushed forward to lap noisily at the water. But as the young shepherd stood over his animals, he heard another sound from behind some nearby bushes—the sound of men's rough laughter.

"Ho, ho! The goddess of Canaan smiles on me tonight! Hebrew shepherd, do you care to try again? Your silver rests easy in my palm!"

"Yes, throw another round! I want my money back. We will see just whom your goddess favors!"

Joseph could not believe his ears. That was his older brother Simeon. Simeon was safe! Maybe the others were, too! Joseph struggled through a thicket of heavy branches, only to tumble into a circle of men crouched on the ground. Gambling stones and coins flew everywhere.

"Wh-what?"

"Who is this youngster?"

Rough hands yanked Joseph to his feet. He looked around at a sea of angry faces. Standing amongst Canaanite shepherds were his older brothers. They were all here—and safe!

"Who are you?" demanded one of the Canaanite men. "Has someone sent you to spy on us?"

"N-no!" the youth stammered. "I am Joseph, son of Israel. When I could not find my brothers, I was worried something bad had happened." He turned to his older brother. "Simeon, you should not be gambling with these pagans! Our family honors the one true living God! What would Father say about this?"

"He will not know if you do not tell him! Make sure that you don't," Simeon snarled, "or I'll—"

"That's enough, brother," Reuben broke in. "You are through with your games for one night. Come, the flocks are waiting."

"But what about my silver? The Canaanites cheated me," Simeon howled. He lunged for the money pouch hanging at the belt of one of the pagan men, his big fists flying.

The Canaanites were only too glad to fight. "Oh, so you think our game stones cheat? Let's see if our knives cheat as well!"

Grabbing Simeon before a fight could begin, the brothers took their flocks and quickly headed for the east. The Canaanites' taunts and cruel laughter echoed after them. But Simeon's temper cooled long before the eleven arrived home the next day. They were just in time for the evening meal. After washing the dust of the hills from their hands and feet, they settled on the soft rug that carpeted their father's large comfortable tent.

The old man looked lovingly at the sons seated around him. Reuben and Simeon, the oldest, were almost grown. Soon they would marry and have children of their own. Then came Gad, Asher, Levi, Judah, Issachar, Zebulun, Dan and Naphtali. Youngest of all were Joseph and Benjamin. Joseph had just this year started working with his brothers, herding the family's many flocks. Benjamin was still a child, barely old enough to leave the women and eat in the men's tent. Lifting his hands toward heaven, the old man, once known as Jacob, now called Israel, prayed.

"My God, God of my father Isaac and his father Abraham, I thank You this day for the gift of sons. May they be a blessing to all the peoples of the earth. And for the bounty of Thy land, of which we are about to eat, we give Thee thanks."

For a few moments, it was quiet as the hungry young men filled their bowls high from the dishes spread before them: dark sticky dates, pungent olives, a rich stew of meat and beans, bread warm from the cooking fire. Israel was a wealthy man, and all in his household ate well. But at last the father turned to his eldest son for a report.

"So tell me, Reuben, do the flocks prosper?"

"Yes, Father. There are many healthy new lambs. And we have kept such close watch, no beasts have stolen any from us."

Israel nodded with satisfaction. "Good, good. But what about the Canaanites? They are such wicked men, I feel they are a greater danger than the wild beasts. Has there been any trouble lately with them?"

Reuben hesitated. "No-o, Father, no—trouble."

"Your tone of voice does not reassure me. Reuben, did something happen on this trip?"

"Nothing, Father. It was nothing." Reuben quickly stuffed a chunk of bread in his mouth.

The old man looked around the circle. "Gad? Naphtali? Did you see anything? Tell me what went wrong!"

But the young men were silent.

That was when little Benjamin piped up. "Ask Joseph, Father! He has sharp eyes! I know he would not miss a thing!"

Israel turned to the seventeen-year-old. "Well, Joseph? Is there trouble with the Canaanites? That is the last thing this family needs!"

Joseph shifted on the thick carpet. He felt Simeon's angry gaze, as the others gave him looks of silent warning. He cleared his throat slowly. What should he say? Should he tell about the gambling game with the pagans? But that was days ago, and they were safe at home now. Surely Simeon and the others would never tangle with the Canaanite men again. It was too dangerous.

"No," he answered at last. "I do not think there will be any trouble with the pagan shepherds, Father. We know better than to get close to them."

Later on that night, when the two youngest brothers were alone in their sleeping tent, little Benjamin peppered Joseph with questions. "What happened out on the hills? I know you saw something. Why can't you tell me, Joseph?

Please, tell me!"

"Hush, small one. If I am going to keep the flocks with our older brothers, I must learn their ways. Yes, I saw something that concerned me, but what of it? To Reuben and Simeon and the others, I am just a youngster, same as you!" With that Joseph rolled over to wrestle affectionately with Benjamin. The two boys rolled and tossed, rumpling the rugs beneath them, shrieking in fun. Finally exhausted, little Benjamin sighed happily and flopped down on his thick mat to sleep. Joseph lay awake a while longer, gazing through the tent door at the night sky.

"Sons as numerous as the stars. . ." he murmured softly. "God will bless our family, and through our offspring, all nations on earth will be blessed."

It was a promise his mother Rachel had taught him, from the time he was a small child. It was the promise given many years ago to Father Abraham when he first began to walk in the ways of the Lord. It was the promise Joseph's own father Israel believed for his tent full of strong young sons.

"I, too, believe in You," Joseph whispered to the sky. "O Lord Most High, be my God, just as You were Abraham's God, and I will honor and serve You all the days of my life."

So Joseph slept.

The brothers stayed in the comfort of their father's tents just long enough to rest the smallest lambs. In a few days they were back out on the hillside. Joseph went with them, once again protesting when they made camp near Canaanite herdsmen.

"Brothers! Let us go to another stream to water our flocks tonight. The water will be cleaner there, and we will have plenty of space to spread our cloaks for sleeping. There are too many Canaanites here for my taste!"

Gad and Asher laughed. "If you would take a taste of the gaming stones, little brother, you would not worry so much about the Canaanites. They are just men, the same as we are! What harm can come of a few little games of chance?"

But Joseph would not listen. "They are pagans, who worship false gods. Their words and their games dishonor the one true living God. And besides, Father has often told us to stay away from them."

Joseph's words of caution fell on deaf ears. His

brothers settled their flocks, then made straight for the pagan camp. Crude laughter and rough talk sounded long into the night. Many coins changed hands as the shepherds gambled and tossed the game stones.

Joseph, curled up in his cloak by the fire, tried hard not to listen when the gamblers called on the Canaanite gods to give them success.

"We are to honor the one true living God, and only Him!" Joseph murmured over and over to himself. "My brothers should not be part of this!"

The next thing Joseph knew, a hand was roughly shaking him awake. It was very early morning, and stars still filled the sky.

"Come, Joseph. We must leave now!"

Joseph's eyes were just slits as he rolled over, but they flew wide open at the sight of Reuben's face.

"Brother! Your nose, your eye! What happened?"

Reuben gave a grunt of disgust. "You were the smart one, to keep apart from the pagans. We never should have tried to beat the Canaanites at their own game. First we lost all our money, then Simeon and Gad started throwing punches. A terrible fight broke out, but thanks be to God, none of us were killed. As it is, we all bear the marks of last night on our bodies. These bumps and bruises will make for a painful trip home."

Joseph hurried to help his injured brothers. He wrapped their swollen hands in strips torn from his own cloak. He fetched cool water to cleanse bloody lips and noses. He took the lead on the way home, keeping a lookout for danger and guiding the flocks so his brothers could have an easier time. Stumbling and limping, the wound-ed men slowly made their way back to their father's tents.

Even though the journey home took several days, the bandages and black eyes were still easy to spot when their father Israel came up the path to meet them. The old man cried out at the sight of their bruised faces.

"A-ei-ei! What is this? I knew trouble was brew-ing! What happened? Hmm, that eye looks bad, Reuben. Zebulun, how did you make it home on that ankle?" Israel's eyes moved from son to son, as he reassured himself that all eleven were safe. "Joseph—where is my Joseph? Surely you older ones protected him! Where is he?"

The seventeen-year-old stepped forward. He

had just seen the last of the sheep into their fold.

"Here I am, Father. Do not worry. The flocks are all here, and I am well."

The old man looked his son up and down, searching for any sign of injury. Seeing only a cloak torn in shreds, Israel clutched Joseph to his chest.

"My son, my son! I would give all my sheep for your safety! Thanks be to God you are alive!"

Joseph rested in his father's arms for a moment, then straightened up, his eyes filled with regret. "Father, I am sorry. I should have told you before. Out in the hills, whenever it is time to stop for the night, we have made our camp near the Canaanite herdsmen. My brothers joke and throw the gaming stones with them. Two times now, there has been some fighting."

Behind Joseph, the brothers began to mutter in protest.

"The young fool!"

"Pay no attention, Father. He is acting like a child!"

"Joseph exaggerates!"

"We can handle the Canaanites!"

The old man whirled to face his older sons,

anger blazing from his eyes. "Gambling? These wounds are from gambling with the Canaanites? You are nearly grown men. I should not have to remind you that the Canaanites have been our enemies; their idol worship is an insult to the God of our father Abraham. Your disobedience amazes me! Go from my sight, all of you, until I decide what to do about the foolishness of my sons!"

Avoiding their father's eyes, the brothers trudged off to their tents, to wash their sore bodies and put on soft robes. Joseph started to follow, but Israel held him back.

"Tell me, my son," the old man spoke softly, in a hurt tone. "Did you win any Canaanite coins? Did your fists find their way to a pagan jaw?"

Joseph's mouth dropped open in surprise. "Father! I would never gamble with the pagans. They dedicate their games to gods made of wood and stone. I have promised to honor only our one true living God. Besides," Joseph laughed sheepishly, "I slept through almost everything. I did not know anything about the fighting until Reuben woke me the next morning."

Israel gently patted his young son's shoulder and sighed. "Your mother Rachel taught you well,

Joseph. Of all my children, you are a true son in faith. How I pray your brothers would come to love God as much as you do!"

The old man's hands explored the ripped threads of Joseph's cloak. "I must see about getting you a new cloak. I noticed bits and pieces of this one wrapped around your brothers' wounds. You are growing into quite a man, my son. Go now, clean yourself. Little Benjamin can hardly wait to see you."

Joseph went to wash up. He was glad he had finally told their father the truth about the gambling, but he dreaded facing his older brothers. Joseph was sure there would be plenty of angry words. He squared his shoulders.

"I must remember what my mother taught me," he murmured to himself. "The Lord always desires the truth."

And with that thought planted firmly in his mind, the young man drew back the flap to the brothers' tent.

A coat fit for a king

CHAPTER 2
Daydreams and Jealousy

The next few days were uncomfortable ones in the tents of Father Israel. Everyone waited to see how he would punish his sons for their reckless behavior. Dealing with pagans was always risky, but to gamble and fight with them was inviting a full-scale war. It was especially dangerous for Israel and his family because they were newcomers to the land. God had promised long ago that some day, all the land would be theirs. Until then, they had to be very careful. Israel was angry that having a little fun seemed more important to his sons than the family's safety. The older brothers' bruises began to mend, but their father kept his distance, refusing to speak even when the family gathered for a meal.

At first, the young men tried to talk and laugh

as usual, but the look on Israel's face stopped them. At last, one night, the old man broke his silence.

"I have spent the last few days thinking," he told his sons. "I have wondered how to teach you obedience, to me, and more importantly, to our God. I have decided your wounds are punishment enough, but I will reward the one son who has respected my commands. Joseph, this is for you!"

Israel handed a bundle tied with twine to his younger son. Joseph fumbled with the knot for a few seconds, but finally got it loosened. Everyone in the tent gasped as the bundle unrolled to reveal a brilliant cloth of red and purple and blue and gold.

"O-h-h! What is it, Joseph? A new blanket?" Benjamin crowded in close to see. The older brothers watched in stony silence.

The youth shook out the colorful cloth. One sleeve, then another, appeared from its folds. It was a coat, a beautiful coat, a coat of many colors.

"Father, I—I do not know what to say—except thank you!" Joseph bowed gratefully before his father, then drew his arms through the sleeves. The coat felt just right on his shoulders. Its two sleeves hung in deep dramatic folds around his wrists. The hem of the garment fell to just above the tops of Joseph's sandals. It was a noble coat indeed.

Joseph turned slowly, watching as the glorious colors of the coat caught the last rays of the evening sun. What a handsome sight he was! The colors of the coat flashed as he twirled around, lighting up his glossy dark hair, bringing a gleam to his dark brown eyes. Joseph's older brothers could only stare, shocked at the sight of the youth in the magnificent coat.

As usual, little Benjamin had something to say. "Look! Look, everybody! Joseph looks like a king! He looks just like a king wearing his royal robe! Look, Joseph will be the king, and I will be his royal advisor!"

Laughing with pleasure, Benjamin made an exaggerated bow before his brother and kissed the hem of the colorful coat.

Joseph and Father Israel laughed with the boy, but his playful words fell like poison on the brothers' hearts.

Levi finally spoke. "What could you have been thinking, Father, to give Joseph a coat like this?

This coat is not fit for a shepherd boy. Look, the sleeves will drag in the mud every time he reaches down to grab a lamb. The coat is so long, he is sure to trip over it when we climb up steep paths. Is an ordinary shepherd's cloak not good enough for him? It has always served well enough for each of us. Father, this coat is not for one who tends smelly sheep. Benjamin is right. A prince would be proud to wear such a coat as this! Why did you waste good money on a garment that Joseph cannot possibly ever use?"

Israel paused a moment before answering. He considered his words carefully, for he knew they would disturb his older sons. "You are right, Levi, when you say that this is a coat fit for a leader. Young as he may be, Joseph already is proving to me that he desires to walk in the ways of righteousness. That is exactly the kind of son I want to lead this family when I have lived out my days on earth and have gone to be with the Lord. Why did I give Joseph the coat? It is simple. He has respected my commands. Would that my older sons were as careful to listen to the words of their old father and obey them."

Taking Joseph with one arm and young

Benjamin with the other, Israel left the tent. The older brothers exploded in anger as soon as their father was out of hearing.

"Did you see that coat? What I would not give for one like that!"

"Why, never in all of his days has our father given something so costly to any one of us! It simply is not fair!"

"Joseph only got that coat because he told tales on us. So we gambled some. Is that such a crime? If that telltale values his new coat, he had better hide it. I can think of plenty of ways a coat like that can get torn up, can't you?"

"Brothers, did you hear what Father said? He intends to make Joseph the head of this family! Reuben is firstborn; he should be head."

"I promise you this—no boy is going to stand around and tell me what to do. Not ever!"

The more the brothers talked, the greater their resentment of Joseph became. Father Israel had intended to plant an important lesson in his older sons' hearts that day. But instead, where his words fell, a seed of jealousy developed. That bad seed grew rapidly, watered by the love and attention Israel poured out on Joseph. Ugly feelings of envy and hatred blossomed in the brothers' hearts each time Joseph put on the coat of many colors. Proud of his grand new garment, the young man wore it often.

"Joseph, you have your new coat on again!" Benjamin exclaimed one morning. "I thought you were going to tend the lambs today. Won't your coat get dirty?"

"Don't worry so, little brother! You can be sure I will take care of my coat. Why would Father have given it to me if he did not want me to wear it? Besides, the bright colors will cheer me up when I'm out on the hills by myself."

Benjamin laughed. "I think you like to show off a little bit, Joseph! Don't let your new coat go to your head. Our brothers still pass all the dirtiest chores around here to you. When Father gives me a coat like yours, I'm going to keep it nice for special occasions."

Joseph ruffled his brother's hair. "Oh, ho! What makes you think you'll ever deserve a coat like mine? You have a lot of growing to do if you're going to keep up with me!" The youth winked at his younger brother. "I'm Father's best son, you know."

"You!" Benjamin hooted. "I'm the youngest. Father loves me best!" The little boy playfully swung his fists in Joseph's direction.

Laughing, Joseph easily dodged and darted out of the tent. Israel's two youngest sons could joke with each other about the fancy coat, but the older brothers did not see it in the same light. Every time Joseph wore the coat, they looked for ways to make his life miserable.

Reuben and Naphtali stood talking one day beside the sheep fold when Joseph came up, bright and cheerful in his colorful coat. The youth smiled and threw his arms around his older brothers' shoulders.

"Brothers, you two have serious faces. Is something wrong with the new lambs? I will sleep out here in the fold tonight if it will help."

The older men frowned.

"Our conversation does not concern you, Joseph. We do not bother to talk to someone who would betray his own brothers."

"I only told the truth! I told Father about the gambling so there would not be any more trouble. I would never betray you to an enemy. You know I am loyal to my family!"

But Reuben and Naphtali would not listen. They walked off, leaving Joseph sputtering.

Shortly after this, the brothers started preparing for a hunting trip in the hills. Usually the flocks kept them so busy, they did not have time for this kind of fun. But their animals were all well. There were no new lambs to tend. It was the season for deer, so laughing and joking, the young men packed their slings and bows. It would be good to bring home some venison for the table.

Joseph brought his gear over to the tent where the older brothers were packing. The laughter suddenly stopped. Issachar frowned at the youth in the brightly colored coat.

"This trip is only for men, Joseph," he said harshly. "We have no spot for boys who are full of themselves. Besides, that coat of yours would scare off all the deer in Canaan!"

Joseph protested, but his older brothers paid no attention. Leaving the youth at the front of the tent, they made their way up the path, singing and shouting as they went. Joseph opened his mouth to ask once more to come, then clamped his lips tightly shut. "No," he thought to himself. "If they don't want me, I won't beg. I will just go do something by myself!"

Despite his brave thoughts, Joseph's feelings were wounded. His older brothers had always been rough with him, but now more than ever. Why? Puzzled and hurt, Joseph began to spend time alone. He would walk the paths near his father's camp for hours at a time, lost in thought. Soon, everyone for miles around knew that the bright splash of color on the hillside was Joseph, Israel's younger son. The daydreamer, they began to call him.

Some time later, the older brothers were out in the field one day, putting up a new fence. It had just rained, and the earth was soft and easy to dig. The men were busy making holes for fenceposts when they saw a flash of red and purple through the bushes.

Gad called to the others. "Quick, Joseph is coming! Asher, bring some mud from that puddle over there. Dump it here in this hole. Dan, get some leaves and twigs. We'll put them over the hole. When Joseph comes along, he'll step on the twigs. Then won't he be surprised!"

The brothers laughed unkindly. They hurried to follow Gad's directions. Soon one of the holes they had dug was filled with mud and hidden by branches. Joseph did not notice anything unusual and stepped right onto the leafy spot. The twigs gave way and Joseph's leg crashed down into the hole. Mud splashed all over the coat of many colors.

"Ha, ha! Look at the daydreamer's fancy coat now!" Gad jeered.

Joseph feebly tried to join in the laughter, but the twinge in his ankle stopped him. Gingerly pulling his leg out of the hole, he tried to wiggle his foot. Ouch! He had twisted it falling, and now it was beginning to swell. He turned to ask for help.

"Brothers, could one of you help me up? I seem to have turned my ankle. If I can get back home and wrap it up tightly, I think it will be all right."

Each one muttering a different excuse, the older brothers turned and walked away. Joseph had to hobble back to his father's tents all by himself. Benjamin found him there a short time later, his foot propped up on a stool.

"Joseph!" he gasped. "What happened?"

When Benjamin heard about the cruel trick the older brothers had played on Joseph, he was angry. "I'm going to Father," he declared. "He needs to know what Gad did to you, Joseph."

But Joseph would hear nothing of it. "No, please. Forget about it, Benjamin. It was just a prank between brothers. They have always played rough games. I'll just rest my foot and keep out of their way. Everything will be fine in a few days, you'll see."

Little Benjamin did as Joseph asked, telling no one about the cruel trick. Joseph stayed in his tent for a week to nurse his tender ankle and to keep out of his brothers' sight. During this time, their hard feelings toward Joseph began to ease. Perhaps they would have disappeared all together, but then something else stirred the hatred again. Joseph began to dream very strange dreams. His foot was almost well when he woke one morning with powerful images filling his head. Joseph got up and threw on his colorful coat. He hobbled over to his father's tent, eager to share what he had seen in his dream. The rest of the family was already eating the morning meal.

"Listen to this, brothers!" he announced in an excited voice. "I had such an odd dream last night, and all of you were in it! I dreamed we were all busy out in the fields, tying stalks of grain into bundles. Suddenly, my bundle flew out of my hands and stood up by itself. Then the bundles all of you had tied gathered in a circle around my bundle and bowed low before it. How funny, that my bundle of grain was king over yours!" And Joseph chuckled to himself over the strange dream.

But the brothers were not amused. Joseph's dream fanned their feelings of jealousy. "So, do you still think of being king? Do you actually think you could rule over us? Haven't you learned by now— we will always be older and smarter and stronger than you. We will never allow you to become king over us!" And they hated him all the more because of the dream.

Joseph could not get the dream out of his mind. What did it mean? Was he really going to rule his brothers one day? Joseph knew that sometimes God spoke through dreams. Could God have a special plan for him? With his father's coat of many colors on his back, and his head full of this proud new idea, Joseph made it very easy for his brothers to despise him all the more.

A short time later, he had a second dream. Once

again, the dream was so vivid that he spoke without thinking of how proud and boastful his words sounded.

"Father, brothers, listen to me! Last night, the sun and the moon and eleven stars were in my dream. And they were all bowing down—to me!" Joseph stared dreamily into space, thinking about his future. "Maybe my dream means that I will be important someday. Maybe I will be a great man, one before whom many people will bow. . ."

Lost in thought, Joseph sighed and pulled the colorful coat tighter around his shoulders. The older brothers snorted in disgust. But Joseph did not hear. He continued to daydream. "When I am rich and powerful, I will buy many coats, even better than this one, enough to wear a different-colored coat every single day. . ."

At Joseph's childish words, sparks of hatred glinted in the older brothers' eyes. Seeing this, Israel quickly took his younger son aside. "Joseph, it is not wise to talk about these odd dreams of yours. Have you stopped to ask yourself how your words sound to your brothers? They think you are bragging about becoming their king someday. It upsets them, and rightly so. Think for a moment. You are the son of a shepherd. How would it ever happen that your brothers and I would bow before you?"

The excitement on Joseph's face faded. "I do not know, Father, but the dream seemed so real to me. Could God be speaking to me? He spoke to you in a dream when you were young, didn't He, Father?" he asked.

Israel paused. It had been so long ago. But he often told his sons the story of how, as a young man, he had dreamed of a staircase that stretched from heaven to earth, with the angels of God going up and down. God Himself had spoken to him that night.

"I am the Lord," God had said, "the God of Abraham and Isaac. The ground you are lying on is yours! I give it to you and to your descendants. Know that I will be with you always, to protect you wherever you go and whatever you do."

For Israel, that dream had been the beginning of a lifetime of great faith in God. Later that evening, alone in his tent, Israel thought once more of the dream he had dreamed so long ago. Through all the years, God had kept His word, in good times and in bad. Israel bowed his head to pray. "Lord, you have blessed me with many sons in my old age. But managing them is a troublesome job. Show me what to do, to help my sons walk faithfully with You and to keep peace in the family."

Israel turned over to go to sleep, but his last thoughts were of his younger son Joseph and those strange dreams of his. Were they a sign of the boy's future? Perhaps, but for now, these dreams only meant trouble for the whole family.

The next day, Israel called Joseph to his tent. "Tomorrow, my son, when your brothers leave to take the flocks to Shechem, you will remain here."

The youth's face crumpled. "Father! Are you punishing me for the words I spoke yesterday? I was only daydreaming. I have to go!"

Israel held up a hand to silence his son, then left.

Alone, Joseph kicked at the carpet with his toe. He could disobey, he thought, and go to Shechem anyway. No, that would only make things worse. It would dishonor God as well as his father. Joseph decided instead to obey.

"I shall stay behind as Father commands," he said to himself. "And I will prove to everyone that of all his sons, I am indeed worthy of his trust."

A battle of lions

CHAPTER 3
Dangerous Journey

In all his seventeen years, Joseph had never worked as hard as he did after his older brothers left for Shechem. It had been difficult to watch them go, but Joseph swallowed his pride and plunged into the tasks that needed attention in and around his father's tents. There were sickly lambs to tend, and fences to repair. There were puppies to train in herding. There were hides to be cut into straps and harnesses to make. There was firewood to gather, and grain to thresh.

Joseph was up before sunrise each morning, helping milk the sheep, heating the large ovens for the day's baking, bringing water from the well.

But for all his hard work, it was not unusual to see the strong, handsome youth stop in the very middle of a job. For a few moments he would stare dreamily into the clouds, his thoughts obviously miles away. After a minute or two, he would dive back into the task at hand, accomplishing work that it normally took two people to do.

During these days, Joseph also spent much time with his little brother. Benjamin was delighted. As the youngest son in Israel's large family, he was always left behind when the older brothers took the flocks to graze in faraway pastures. His father kept him close by his side and loved this youngest son dearly, but Benjamin longed to be with the brother closest to his own age. When Reuben and the others left for Shechem, Joseph taught Benjamin how to make a powerful shepherd's slingshot and how to throw a spear. The two spent hours running foot-races and climbing rocks on the hills near by.

At night, when the two brothers settled in their tent to sleep, Joseph told Benjamin stories about their mother, Rachel. She had died when Benjamin was a baby, and he could not remember her at all. Joseph described their mother's great beauty and how their father had worked fourteen years to have her as his wife.

Benjamin sighed happily. "Father must have loved her very much," he said.

"Yes, he did," Joseph replied. "And that is why he loves the two of us so, because we are all he has left of Rachel. You and I are blood brothers, Benjamin. The blood that runs in my veins also runs in yours. Only the two of us share the same mother and father. Israel is the father of all our older brothers, but their mothers were Leah, Zilpah and Bilhah."

Benjamin looked puzzled. "So, does that make us different from Reuben and Simeon and Gad and the rest? I do not understand."

Joseph chuckled. "Not different, just blessed. Of all Father's wives, our mother loved the Lord the most, I think. That is why she taught me to love Him when I was a small boy, before she died. That is what I want to teach you, too. For our mother's and father's sake, we both must try very hard to walk in the ways of righteousness. No complaining, always helpful, obedient. Father is growing old, and the one thing he wants above all, Benjamin, is to see his sons walking in the ways of the Lord."

Benjamin looked serious. "I will try, Joseph, I promise. It is so hard, though, being the youngest. I will never be old enough to go with you and the others!"

Joseph laughed. "Oh, yes, you will, and there will be plenty of work for you to do. Then you will wish to be a child again!" Joseph's voice grew serious. "But when it is hard to wait, try praying, little brother. Our God hears all who call on Him, and He will give you patience."

"What do you pray for, Joseph?" Benjamin was curious.

It was a long moment before Joseph replied. When he finally spoke, his answer was short. "To be a very great man someday. Now go to sleep!"

In just a few minutes, the sound of soft, little-boy snores filled the tent. Joseph smiled to himself. How he loved Benjamin! It was good for them to have this time together, Joseph thought, even though it still hurt, having to stay behind while the older brothers went to Shechem.

"I've always wanted to see the northern country. I wonder what it is like up there. . ." Immediately, Joseph's head filled with imagined scenes. He could just picture himself, crossing rough streams and climbing steep rocks, beating off wild animals with a stick, rescuing lambs stranded on a hillside. It was not long before his deeper snores joined Benjamin's.

During these days while the older brothers were away, Father Israel kept a watchful eye on Joseph. He noticed that Joseph spent some time alone each day, thinking and talking to himself. But he also saw how cheerfully the lad worked around the tents, helping anyone who needed a hand, setting a good example for little Benjamin. Israel sighed. It was so hard to raise godly, obedient sons. Joseph certainly was growing into a handsome young man. The sight of the tall youth in the coat of many colors flooded Israel's heart with love. But what of Joseph's active imagination, and those troubling dreams at night? And when would the boy learn to consider his words before he spoke? Israel took his concerns to the Lord.

"Lord God," Israel asked in his prayers, "what plan do you have for Joseph? Of all my sons, I feel he is the one to lead this family when I am gone. Help the older ones come to love Joseph as I do. Keep Joseph from getting caught up in his wild dreams. Silence any words that sound boastful, Lord, before they leave his lips. Grow Joseph up to be a man, and help him learn to always depend on You."

Time passed, and the day came when Israel looked for his older sons to return from Shechem with their flocks. Each afternoon, the old man sat outside his tent, listening for the tink-tink of sheep bells, searching for familiar figures on the horizon. But there was no sign of the ten men. Finally, Israel could no longer hide his worries. He summoned Joseph.

"As you know," Israel said, "I sent your brothers to graze the flocks near Shechem. They should have returned home by now. I am going to send you, Joseph, to see if all is well with them. Bring word back to me of how my sons and my flocks are doing."

Joseph could barely keep his feet from dancing. Shechem! He was going to get to go to Shechem after all! But he contained his excitement and bowed his head before Israel.

"Very well, Father. I will leave at first light tomorrow. And I promise I will not stop until I have found my brothers!"

The old man lifted Joseph's head to look into his

eyes. "It is a difficult journey of fifty miles, my son," Israel said soberly. "There are many dangers along the way. I will pray to the Lord to protect you. You must stay alert at all times. No daydreaming. It could cost you your life. Do you understand, my son?"

Joseph nodded gravely. "Do not worry, Father. I will never take my eyes off the path!"

With a pouch of food at his belt and a sturdy staff in his hand, Joseph headed north for Shechem early the next morning. Israel watched him leave with a heavy heart. Of all his sons, it was so hard to send this one out into the world. Trouble, the old man knew, could be found in every turn of the road. Israel loved all his sons, but in his heart, he believed this one somehow was special. "Go with him, Lord!" the father prayed.

Turning back to wave one last time, Joseph headed north. He moved quickly, finding joy in each step that he took. How good it felt to be out in the hills on his own. And what a beautiful land Canaan was. All that day and the next Joseph followed familiar trails. He had been this way many times before with his flocks. But by late afternoon of the third day, Joseph reached new territory.

Here, all the rocky hills looked very different. They cast strange shadows that made the young man uneasy. Joseph approached each fork in the road with great caution. Which trail would lead him to Shechem? What dangers might lie ahead?

Frightening images crowded into Joseph's head. In his imagination, he saw huge beasts behind every bush. Was that a bear over there, he wondered? Could the tracks on the path be the footprints of a wolf? That boulder was the perfect place for robbers to hide. Then, when he was not looking, they would jump out and attack him. . . The young man found himself daydreaming instead of watching the road ahead.

"Stop it!" Joseph told himself firmly. "Stop thinking these thoughts. You are scaring yourself! Trust in God, and pay attention. Shechem cannot be too much further."

Joseph quickened his step and kept his eyes on the trail. A little while later, exhausted from the strains of traveling in this strange territory, Joseph stopped at a large clearing. It was growing too dark to see well, so the young man decided to rest for the night. He propped his staff against a tree and wrapped up in his colorful cloak. Then he stretched himself out under the spreading branches. The moon had already risen and it shone brightly, lighting up the bushes that surrounded the clearing. They glowed eerily in the moonlight. Joseph ignored his uneasy feelings and closed his eyes.

"Watch over me, Lord," he mumbled wearily, "while I am so far from my father's tents. Keep my mind from running astray. No nightmares or wild ideas. . .Just thoughts of. . .You, Lord. . ."

Joseph was almost asleep when an angry cry from deep in the wilderness made him sit up, wide awake. The youth listened intently. What could it be, that cry? Whatever it was, it was big and fierce and angry. The cry sounded from far off in the bushes again. Joseph's heart pounded in his chest as he strained to remember stories his brothers had told of beasts in the hills. Then, suddenly, Joseph knew. Even though he had never heard one before, he knew. This was a lion!

"Oh God, my God!" Joseph panted, "protect me from this beast! Give me strength and courage, and save me, Lord!"

The youth listened fiercely, hardly daring to breathe. He heard another roar, this time much closer. The cry, somehow, was higher, as if the lion were roaring on a different note. Joseph leaned his ear in the direction of the sound, straining to listen. There, over in the bushes not too far from the very tree where he waited, he heard the same high roar. Then Joseph suddenly realized. It was not the same lion he had heard before! There were two lions, an old male and a younger one. Two lions were roaring in the night, each warning the other to leave the area. From his brothers' tales, Joseph knew that lions lived alone. They would protect their territory, fighting to the death if necessary. Any moment now, the first lion would find the younger intruder and attack. Joseph's heart felt as if it would burst from his chest. It was dangerous enough to face one lion, but two?

"Lord, Oh, Lord, save me!" he breathed again.

Joseph reached into the folds of his cloak and felt for the sling that, as a shepherd, he always carried. He looked up at the large tree branches overhead, and a thought came to him. He grabbed up his staff and awkwardly climbed the tree, draping himself over a branch that hung out over the bushes. Next, he wedged the staff between two limbs, an easy reach away. Then he pulled out his sling and fixed a stone from the pouch in the leather strap. There, he was ready. If either lion came any nearer, he would aim his stone at the spot right between their eyes. He listened again and waited.

Never had Joseph faced down lions before. He had often scared foxes or wild dogs away from his sheep, but never a lion. Joseph recalled his older brothers telling of the larger beasts that attacked the flocks. Now he tried to remember all they had said. Oh, how he wished they were here with him now! As he sat perched uncomfortably in the tree, a terrible thought suddenly occurred to him. Lions could climb! If either beast saw him up in the tree, or caught his scent, it could claw its way up and get him. He could use his staff to beat the lion off, but it would not be much protection. Joseph looked around in the shadowy moonlight for a better place to hide. There was none.

"One shot, Lord," he prayed. "Let me get one shot off before the lions know I am here. If I could just kill one, perhaps the other would be frightened and run away."

Time seemed to stand still. Joseph waited

motionless up in the tree. His muscles cramped and his ears ached from straining to listen. He heard the deep roar again, much closer this time. The younger lion, rustling in the bushes near Joseph's tree, answered with a roar of his own. The cry sounded almost like a man's scream, full of pain and rage. At any moment, Joseph sensed, the battle between the two lions would begin.

He peered into the darkness, desperately trying to catch a glimpse of either beast. If only he knew which of the bushes they would come from, he could whirl his sling when the two animals sprang at each other's throat. Then, in the blink of an eye, moving so fast in the moonlight that Joseph could see no more than a blur of bushy manes and muscular bodies, the lions burst into the clearing. With horrible screams and snarls, they leaped at each other, their enormous jaws snapping. The lions rolled over and over, growling and ripping and clawing. From high in the tree, Joseph watched motionless. Even the smallest movement, he knew, would draw the lions' attention to him.

There was a pause in the battle below. The younger lion had pinned the older one to the ground for a slight second, but with a twist of his powerful body, the older lion got away. He stalked over to the edge of the clearing and turned to face his opponent. The huge creature paced back and forth, shaking his mane at the young lion as if to say, "This is my kingdom. How dare you come here? I will teach you a painful lesson!"

Then, with a mighty roar, the great beast charged, sinking his teeth deeply into the younger lion's rump. The smaller animal screamed in agony. He twisted and turned. He pawed frantically at his enemy, struggling to get away. Overhead, Joseph found himself digging his fingernails into the bark of the branch. "You can do it, young one," he silently cheered. "Get away from that beast! Get away and run! Run, and never come back here! Find yourself another place to be king!"

Even as Joseph thought these words, the young lion sprang free from his captor's claws. Limping and bleeding, he ran from the clearing and disappeared into the darkness. The older lion watched him go, but made no effort to chase after him. Instead, the beast padded around the clearing, swinging his head from side to side, reclaiming the territory as his alone.

Joseph watched, almost forgetting his fear in his fascination with the powerful creature. The beast beneath him was huge. The moonlight highlighted its muscular body and massive paws as the lion paced across the clearing. A single swipe, Joseph realized, was all it would take to kill a sheep or seriously injure a man. The lion suddenly stopped right under Joseph's tree, lifted its huge head and roared. The long pointed teeth glinted fearsomely in the great yawning mouth. Joseph's ears rang with the thundering roar. He felt faint, as if he might topple out of the tree at any moment.

"What a wondrous creature you have made, O God! Only You are more powerful than this great beast of the wilderness."

In fear and trembling, Joseph silently worshipped the Lord. At last, the lion glided into the bushes, his big paws stepping so gently, they did not even rustle the dry leaves on the ground. As Joseph watched him disappear into the shadows, he wondered how long he had sat motionless up in the tree. Moving only slightly, he flexed his muscles and relaxed his grip on the branch. Oh, how it hurt to move! But Joseph knew he had been blessed.

"Thank you for sparing my life, Lord! Truly You are my protector and my hiding place! Who could stand up before the power of lions like those?" Joseph was suddenly filled with new understanding. "My brothers! They have faced lions many times. What brave men they are! I never realized it before."

The young man sat up in the tree for the rest of the night, his sling ready by his side should either lion return. But Joseph heard no more roaring, and after long hours of watchfulness, he finally dozed off, his head resting on the rough bark of the tree. By early morning, he was back on the path, determined to reach Shechem and locate his brothers as quickly as he could. Father was right to be worried, with lions roaming the region.

It was not long before the dusty landscape began to change. Grass beside the trail grew thick and green. Songbirds flitted through treetops. Even the air smelled fresher. Joseph picked up his pace. The town of Shechem, with its large spring of clear water, had to be nearby. He studied the fields as he walked. Reuben and Zebulun and

Asher and the others, where were they?

"That is quite a colorful coat you are wearing, my young stranger," a voice called out. "Are you searching for someone?"

Joseph turned and looked into the friendly face of a man carrying a well-worn shepherd's staff. "Yes, I have been sent to find ten men from Hebron and their flocks, sir." Joseph told him. "They are my brothers. Have you seen them?"

The man rested his chin on the staff while he thought. "Hmm. There were some strangers who passed this way a few days ago. There may have been ten of them. They certainly had plenty of sheep. Those animals nearly drank Shechem spring dry! But young man, they are not here now."

Joseph's heart leaped into his throat. Immediately, he could see images of his brothers wounded and bleeding in his mind.

"Sir, tell me, please— what happened? Why did they leave? Were they all right? Were they well when you last saw them? Please, sir, I must know!"

"Calm down, young stranger. I never said there was anything wrong. I think they just wanted to look around a little more. Said they were heading northwest, to Dothan."

"Dothan? I have never heard of that place. How far is Dothan from here?"

The man scratched his head. "Oh, a fair distance. About twenty miles, I'd say."

Joseph's heart sank. Twenty miles! He would have to travel another two days before he could find his brothers. He quickly turned to go.

"Young stranger, wait!" the shepherd called after him. "Why do you hurry so? Rest here with my family for the night and pick up your journey tomorrow!"

"Thank you, kind sir," Joseph called back. "But I must go now. My brothers may be in danger, and my aged father is very worried. I must find them and bring word of their safety as soon as I can."

Joseph chuckled as he lifted his hand to wave farewell. What a tale he could have told if he had spent the night. But storytelling would just have to wait for now. Joseph hurried north, more determined than ever to locate his brothers.

"I must find them," he told himself, "before the lions do."

Trapped in a well

CHAPTER 4
Given Up for Good

Twenty miles away, on the hills outside of Dothan, Joseph's brothers grazed their flocks. The time away from their father's tents had been peaceful and productive, with little to trouble them. They had found many green pastures, and the sheep were fat and healthy.

Reuben sighed as he poked at their campfire. "Tomorrow we must turn back for home," he told his brothers. "We have stayed away longer than we should have. Our father is surely troubled about our safety."

Simeon snorted. "You are always the worrier, Reuben. We are grown men. Father knows we can take care of ourselves!"

The brothers had not yet moved from the fire when one of them spotted a strange bit of color bobbing far down the road.

"Look there!" Gad pointed. "How odd it appears, that bit of red and purple moving toward us. It reminds me of the special coat our father gave to Joseph. Could that be our younger brother, so far away from home?"

At first, the others just laughed.

"Your eyes are playing tricks on you. Joseph is home right where he belongs, Gad," they teased. "Right by Father's side! Besides, why would Israel let his favorite son risk his life out on these 'dangerous' hills?"

But as the splash of brilliant color moved steadily closer, they all stared. At last Naphtali spoke, resentment clear in his voice.

"It is indeed Joseph, the great daydreamer, the one before whom we must all bow someday. Do you think he has had any more grand dreams, brothers?"

"I should like to give him some evil dreams," Asher muttered through clenched teeth, "with this!" And the husky young man shook his fist angrily in Joseph's direction.

The others muttered their agreement. How they hated this younger brother!

Simeon spoke softly. "Now is our chance, while we are so far from our father's tents. I say we should kill the troublemaker and be done with him. It will be simple. Look, we can tell our father that wild animals ate him. There have been plenty of reports of lions seen lately. Israel will never suspect a thing."

Then the brothers all began to speak at once. Each one had a different idea of how to torment Joseph. Reuben held up a hand for silence.

"Brothers, brothers, calm yourselves," he urged. "I, too, am weary of this daydreamer's big talk. But he is our flesh and blood. Rather than commit murder, let us simply throw him into that dry well over there. With no food and water, he will die in a few days and we will be finished with him forever."

The others thought for a moment, then agreed.

"Good, so it's settled then," Reuben said. "I will go now and check on our flocks we left on the far hill. When Joseph arrives, give him no hint of our plan. Then, after I return this evening, when he suspects nothing, we will put him in the well."

Satisfied with the compromise, Reuben left. In spite of his words to his brothers, Reuben's intentions were good. As the oldest of Israel's sons, he was in charge. He knew that if his brothers harmed Joseph in any way, their father would never forgive them. He could not let that happen. But Reuben lacked the courage to stand up to the other nine. Instead, when he was with his brothers, he acted as if he, too, wanted to get rid of Joseph. Later on, he promised himself, when his brothers had moved on with the flocks, he would secretly return to the well and rescue his father's favorite.

Far off down the road, Joseph was daydreaming. For two long days, he had hurried along the trail from Shechem to Dothan. But now, as his feet grew weary, his mind began to wander.

"Just wait until Father hears about the lions I faced down! From now on, he will be sure to send me on important trips, when the family needs supplies from somewhere far away. I think I make a fair traveler, one who is brave and adventurous. After all, I have come all this way on my own, with no one to guide me. Can any of my older brothers say they have done the same thing? They always travel together. Who knows. . .? Someday I might set out for foreign lands. What it would be like to see the Negev desert, or to travel down the mighty Euphrates? I have heard there are great cities beyond the hills of Canaan, like Nineveh and Babylon and Ur."

"Look how slowly he walks, brothers! He is day-dreaming again. He will walk into a tree if he does not keep his eyes on the path! And he is wearing that coat. Oh-h-h, just the sight of it makes my blood boil!"

From the next hill, the brothers watched as Joseph slowly made his way nearer and nearer. Without Reuben there to calm them, their tempers flared. They forgot the agreement to wait until evening to deal with Joseph. Once again, Simeon, the impulsive one, led the way. He jumped to his feet and started quickly down the trail toward his younger brother. The others followed.

It was not long before Joseph looked up. While the men were still a good ways off, he caught sight of them. The tired youth quickened his pace, looking forward to a happy reunion. Joseph grinned. He could not wait to tell his brothers about the battle between the two lions. Then, after a hot meal and a good night's rest beside his brothers' campfire, he would head for home. Traveling alone, without sheep to slow him, he would reach his father's tents long before they did. How glad Israel would be to receive good news about his sons.

Joseph waved. "Simeon! Gad! It is Joseph, your brother Joseph. Oh, I am relieved you are safe. Father and I were worried! Asher, Zebulun, it's me, Joseph! Wait until you hear what I saw on my journey here!"

Joseph began to run toward the men who came down the road to meet him. He waved and shouted more greetings. He did not notice the dark expressions on his brothers' faces.

"Issachar, it is so good to see you and Dan— ouch! Stop, brothers, you are hurting me! Stop, that is my good coat! What are you doing? Where are you taking me?"

Without a word, the brothers stripped the coat of many colors from Joseph's back. They gripped his arms tightly and forced him to walk in front of them. In his confusion, Joseph stumbled and almost fell. But Issachar's iron grip shoved Joseph forward. The brothers did not speak until they reached a well that stood at the edge of the clearing. There had not been any water in the well for a long time, and the bottom was dry and covered with leaves and twigs.

Forcing Joseph down on the rock wall that surrounded the well, Simeon growled. "So, how does it feel to bow before your own brothers, Joseph? Show us how low you can go!" And with a great shove, Simeon pushed his younger brother into the deep dry pit.

"A-ah-ahh-hh!" Joseph fell rapidly. As he tumbled down, the rough stones that lined the inside of the well scraped raw places on his arms and legs.

He landed with a bone-jarring thud at the bottom. For an endless moment, Joseph's head spun and spun. He gulped, trying to force air back into his lungs. Gingerly, he unfolded his crumpled arms and legs and picked himself up. Blinking in the sudden darkness, Joseph turned to look back up at the top of the well. There, outlined in brilliant sunlight, were the angry faces of his brothers, staring down.

"What is wrong?" Joseph called to them. "Have I done something to make you mad? Or is this your idea of fun? Help me up! Please, this is not funny. My knees and elbows are bleeding. My head hurts, and I cannot breathe. Just help me get out. I won't say a thing about this little prank to Father or anyone else, I promise! Where's Reuben? He will help me, I know it. Reuben? Re-u-ben! It's me, Joseph! Come help me! The others have thrown me in this well. Help! Please, I am your brother. You cannot let this happen to me. Help!"

But none of the brothers had anything to say to the one they despised so. After staring down at Joseph for a long moment, they moved away silently, one by one. The young man at the bottom of the well continued to scream and call for help, but they ignored his cries. Instead, each brother suddenly found something important he had "forgotten" to do. Judah and Levi picked up sticks and began whittling new whistles. Asher and Zebulun checked the supplies, tightening ropes and repacking pouches. Dan went looking for the wild plants he used to make a healing ointment, while Simeon, Issachar and Naphtali stretched out for a nap by the fire. For a long time, the screams from the well were loud and angry, but as the afternoon wore on, Joseph's voice grew hoarse and weak. He did not stop calling, but the brothers found it easier and easier to ignore him.

After a time, they started to prepare their evening meal, threading chunks of meat on sticks to cook over the coals. The late afternoon breeze carried the smell down to Joseph, and he renewed his pleas from the bottom of the well.

"Dan, Naphtali, please! Do not leave me here! Help me out, brothers. For the love of God and our father Israel, help me, please! Zebulun! Issachar! Please, oh, please get me out! I'm hungry!"

The men eyed each other sheepishly. Judah finally spoke. "I can't stand it, brothers. Joseph's cries tear at my heart. Should we really do this thing and leave him there to die?"

Simeon snorted. "Don't tell me your heart is softening with pity. Just think how Father favors him. And remember how Joseph dreams of ruling over us. If we don't do this now, we will have to live under our little brother's proud gaze for the rest of our lives. I refuse to do that!"

Zebulun spoke. "But Simeon, the boy's cries are almost too much to bear. How much longer do we have to stay here and listen to him? Let us leave at once!"

The others chimed in. "Yes, yes! Let's leave now!"

"We cannot go yet. Reuben has not returned with the rest of the flocks," Simeon reminded them. "We must stay here until he comes from the far pasture. But at least we can move away from this spot. Let us go to the other side of the hill. Reuben will still find us easily, and we won't have to listen to—that!"

Simeon jerked his head in the direction of the well, where pitiful sobs now rose into the evening air. The nine men wasted no time gathering up their things and moving around to the other side of the grassy slope. There, they could no longer hear their brother's pleas. Judah, staring out into the evening shadows suddenly pointed to the valley that stretched below.

"Brothers, look! There, down the road, it is a caravan, coming this way!" He jumped excitedly to his feet and peered into the distance. "By the look of the packs on those donkeys, they must be traders. Brothers, I have an idea. We can sell Joseph to them! Why have his death on our hands, when instead we can make ourselves some easy money?"

The others immediately agreed. So as the traders approached, Joseph's brothers ran back to the well. Quickly, they let down a rope and pulled their brother up.

Thrashing and kicking, Joseph struggled against the strong arms that held him. His feet seemed to fly in all directions at once, landing sharp kicks on his brothers' shins.

Unable to jerk free, he choked and sputtered, spitting out sand and bits of leaves. As soon as he could speak, hurt, angry words poured from his mouth.

"Why? Why would you do this to me? Do you all hate me so much? What is it you wa—"

Joseph's screams were cut short by the bit of dirty cloth Judah shoved into his mouth. For the first time since he had been pulled from the well, Joseph stopped struggling long enough to look around. His eyes widened when he saw the strangers at Simeon's side. The foreigners stared back at Joseph, looking him up and down. With a grunt of satisfaction, one of the men reached for a moneybag at his belt. Joseph watched intently as the trader withdrew some coins and placed them in his older brother's hand.

Seventeen, eighteen, nineteen, twenty, Joseph counted to himself. Twenty pieces of silver. Why, that was the price of a common slave!

Desperately, Joseph whirled to look at the brothers who held his arms. What was going on?

But no explanations came. Instead, the brothers shoved Joseph forward and he went sprawling in the dirt at the traders' feet. Before he realized what was happening, the foreigners had picked him up and slung him onto one of their donkeys. They tied his hands to the pack saddle. With a shout and the crack of a whip, the caravan began to move. Joseph's head reeled. His brothers had done the unthinkable! They had sold him, a descendant of Abraham, Israel's favorite son, into slavery!

Joseph's donkey lurched forward, and the young man's neck snapped back painfully. But he twisted around in the saddle until he could see his brothers, standing in the dusty road. How could they do this? How could they hate him so much?

Choking on tears, Joseph strained against the ropes binding his wrists. He shook his head furiously from side to side to free his chin from the cloth that covered his mouth. It did not budge. Joseph screamed any way. The sounds that came from deep within his throat were the howls of a wounded animal. The words in his mind were those of a young man fighting for his life.

"No, no, not a slave! I will be no one's slave! I am Joseph, son of Israel and Rachel, son of promise and blessing. I will never be a slave! O God in Heaven, is there no one who will hear and help me? No! No! Help me, God! Save me!"

The donkey plodded on. Joseph's brothers stood in the middle of the road and watched. Even when they could no longer see, they stayed rooted to the spot.

At last Judah spoke. "Well, brothers, it is done. We are rid of Joseph. We will never have to listen to his boastful words again. Now all we have to do is convince Father that his son was killed by lions."

"No, Judah, you are wrong. There is something we must do before we go home to father," Issachar said softly. "Look who is coming, behind you. It is our brother Reuben, with the flocks from the far pastureland. What do you think he will say when he learns what we have done?"

Condemned to prison

CHAPTER 5
An End and a Beginning

"Where is he? Tell me, what have you done with Joseph?" Reuben raged. "He is not in the well. I have just come from there. Where is he?"

No one answered. It was later that evening, and the brothers huddled close to the glowing coals of their campfire. Reuben startled them when he stepped out of the darkness into the light. His brothers gasped in surprise, then quickly turned their eyes away.

Immediately, Reuben knew something was wrong. He reached across the circle and jerked Simeon to his feet.

"Tell me now, brother. Where is Joseph?"

Simeon coolly returned the gaze. "If you cared so much for the boy, you should not have left to check on the flocks. While you were gone, we settled the problem of Joseph, once and for all."

Simeon pulled free from his older brother and walked off. Reuben whirled to face the others, panic in his voice.

"Tell me, please! What have you done?" he begged. "I am the oldest son. Father will hold me responsible if we do not return with Joseph. I know you are very angry, but I cannot let you hurt him. I was planning to bring him out of the well in a day or two, after he had learned his lesson."

Reuben stopped and looked anxiously into his brothers' faces. "But now Joseph is not there. You must tell me what you have done with him. Is he—" Reuben choked on the words—"is he—dead?"

Judah tossed a stick in the fire. "Stop worrying, Reuben. Joseph is not dead, just gone from our lives forever. A caravan of traders from the north passed by while you were gone. Our proud younger brother is now on his way with them—to Egypt, to become a slave. Those grand day-dreams of his did not mean a thing!"

Reuben groaned. He ripped at his cloak until it hung in shreds. He paced around the lit campfire like a madman. "Gone? Our father's favorite son is gone? Where shall I go now? Father will never want to look on me again! I am the eldest, the one in charge. I should have known better than to go off and leave you. This never should have happened!"

Reuben raged long into the night. At last, to calm him, the others sat down and planned what they would tell their father when they returned home. Together, they came up with a clever plan.

Dan held out Joseph's colorful coat. "It is good that we kept this. Tomorrow, we can kill a goat from the flock and sprinkle its blood on the coat. Father will think it is Joseph's blood."

Naphtali grabbed a sharp stick. "And see here," he added, poking some holes in the coat. "This makes it look as if a large beast had clawed our poor brother."

Finally, even Reuben was satisfied with the plan. The brothers bedded down beside the fire and woke early the next morning. Before starting for home, they readied the colorful coat, spoiling its brilliant colors with bloody stains and long rips.

"You see now, Reuben, how easy this all has been?" Simeon asked. "Father will never guess what really happened to his precious Joseph, and we won't have to listen to that braggart, ever again!"

So taking the bloody rag in their arms, the brothers headed for home. While they were still far away, Father Israel spotted the colorful coat. He flew down the path to meet them.

"Joseph, Joseph, where is my Joseph? Why do you carry his coat? What has happened to him?" The old man grabbed the striped garment from his sons and held it up. Blood stains covered what was left of the coat, speaking of terrible tragedy.

"Father, we found this out on the hills, near a lion's cave." Asher said. "Did you send Joseph out to meet us?"

Israel clutched the stained garment to his chest. "My son! My Joseph! Lions must have torn him to pieces. Oh, Joseph!" He sobbed and collapsed suddenly on the ground. The brothers rushed to help him up, but the old man refused to move. For hours he sat in the dust, weeping and crying out to God. Finally, the servants got him into his tent. He stayed there for seven days.

During all that time, Israel refused to eat. He ripped huge holes in his clothes and rubbed ashes on his head to symbolize his great sorrow. He did not comb his hair, but let it fall, loose and tangled around his face. At different times of day, one or another of his children would stop by his tent to comfort him. It did little good.

"Father, you must eat. You are too old to go without food like this. You will make yourself sick," Naphtali said.

"Grandfather," sweet little Serah called from the door of the tent, "see what Mother has made for you—honey pastries! Won't you try a bite?"

"Look, Father, at the twin lambs that were born yesterday." Gad said. "God is blessing us with many new births this season."

"I will sing a song, Father," young Benjamin offered. "I miss Joseph terribly, too. Maybe the singing will help both of us feel better."

"Father, we know you loved Joseph very much," Judah said, "and that your sorrow is great. But it has been seven days now. Is it not time to dry your eyes and remember that you still have eleven other sons?"

Judah's words roused Israel from his weeping. The old man stood and roared at his son. "I will die," Israel cried. "I will go to my grave before ever I stop mourning for my son, my Rachel's

Joseph." With these words, Israel began once more to be with his family.

Many many miles away, on the road to Egypt, Joseph's tears were also coming to an end. Exhausted from weeping, the young man realized he had better prepare himself for the future.

For the first two days, he had screamed at the traders whenever they came near him. He shouted insults about his brothers, shrieking that he would never be anyone's slave. He strained against the ropes that held him on the donkey until his wrists were raw and bloody. He also refused to eat. But at last Joseph realized he had a choice to make. He could fight slavery and die, or he could look for some way to live with this terrible thing that his brothers had done.

"O Lord God, strengthen me," Joseph prayed. "Go with me into this strange land. If I must be a slave, help me do my duties well. And someday, Lord, let me see my father and Benjamin again."

The Midianite traders who had bought Joseph were heading south to Egypt. Their donkeys were packed with bundles of sweet-smelling spices, balm and myrrh. As the men conversed in their strange language, Joseph could not help but listen with interest. Soon, he could say a few of their words and phrases himself, enough to ask questions.

"What kind of tree is that?"

"How did you train these donkeys?

"What is myrrh used for?

"How long before we reach Egypt?"

The traders were impressed. Yes, they nodded to each other, this strong alert young man would bring an excellent price at the slave auction. After long dusty days on the road, the caravan arrived at its destination. Just as the traders expected, the interest in Joseph was keen. Several wealthy merchants and Egyptian officials wanted to purchase the youth.

Although Joseph knew the traders would sell him when they arrived in Egypt, he was not prepared for the humiliation of the auction. He was led, along with other captives, to a central square. There, the auctioneer took charge, and pushed those who were to be sold into a line. Modest young girl or dried-up old man, it did not matter; the auctioneer examined each one so he would know the proper price to ask. Women gasped and frightened children cried when the man poked his fingers in their mouths or ran his hands rudely over their bodies to see if they were healthy. When the auctioneer was satisfied the slaves were fit to sell, he motioned to the buyers who waited at the edge of the square.

One man yanked Joseph's tunic open to inspect the youth's firm muscles. Another grabbed at his ear and peered into it. Other buyers asked him questions in the curious-sounding Egyptian language. Joseph had no idea what they were asking, but he spoke to each one, first in a stream of Hebrew, then with a few words of Midianite. "Lord," he prayed silently in the times when no one was looking him over, "I feel lower than one of my father's sheep. Please, let this awful day pass quickly!"

Lord Potiphar watched Joseph closely from the edge of the crowd. He noticed the youth's self-control as people poked and prodded him. He saw the gleam of intelligence in Joseph's eye as the young man puzzled over the foreign words he heard. Yes, Potiphar told himself, that slave just might prove to be an excellent addition to his household.

After an hour, the bidding began. The price for

Joseph quickly rose as several made their offers.

"Six lengths of linen for the young Hebrew!"

"No, the lad is worth more! Here is a sack of the finest wheat in all of Egypt!"

"I will give two milk cows, twenty laying hens and ten geese for the boy."

"This gold and turquoise ring says that he is mine!"

It was Potiphar, captain of Pharoah's palace guard, who spoke last. When all had made their offers, Potiphar's bid proved to be the highest. The officer pulled the young man from the line and motioned Joseph to follow as he threaded his way through the crowded streets. Joseph's eyes grew wide as his new master led the way to a magnificent house. It was far from the noisy slave market, and surrounded by a pleasant garden. Children played there as servants bustled in and out.

What a wealthy man my owner must be, Joseph marveled to himself. Why, all of Abraham's descendants would not fill half the rooms in this great house!

A servant met Joseph at the door and directed him to the back of the compound. There, the older man took Joseph's long soiled tunic and gave him a short linen skirt instead. Joseph looked at it, puzzled. The man laughed and showed him how to wrap it around his waist in the style of a proper Egyptian slave. Next, the servant cut Joseph's long hair, trimming it straight above his eyebrows, and straight again down by his ears and around the back of his neck. The man even shaved off the new whiskers Joseph had just begun to grow. Next, he led the youth out to a pool in the garden and motioned that he could wash himself there.

When Joseph bent down to the water, a strange face stared back. Joseph's heart sank. Even if Israel came all the way to Egypt to look for him, his father would never recognize him. Without his hair and his shepherd's tunic, no one would ever know Joseph was a descendant of the great Abraham. "Oh, God of my fathers," the young man silently prayed by the pool, "I look like a pagan Egyptian. But I am still Joseph, son of Israel, son of Jacob and Isaac and Abraham. And I will always honor you as my God. Be with me now, Lord. Bless me in this strange land, and someday, let me see my family again."

Those first days and weeks in Potiphar's house passed quickly. There was so much to learn, so much that was different from anything Joseph knew as a Hebrew shepherd. He had a new language to master, and strange new customs to follow. Lord Potiphar was patient with his new slave, for he saw great potential in him.

As soon as Joseph could speak a few words in Egyptian, Potiphar sent him to buy food and supplies for the large household. Joseph was surprised to learn that none of the merchants in Egypt dealt in coins. Instead, they bartered with their customers, trading a large bunch of grapes for a handful of barley, a string of freshly caught fish for a pinch of spice, eggs for a scroll. Joseph enjoyed dealing with the trades-people, striking a fair bargain.

For their part, the merchants liked the pleasant young slave who came on Potiphar's business. He always treated them with respect and never tried to cheat. Soon, the woman who sold vegetables would tuck away the freshest beans for Joseph, and the linen merchant would leave extra on the lengths of cloth he delivered to Potiphar's house.

On his daily visits to the marketplace, Joseph

always took a few minutes to stop by the table where the scribes worked. Most people in the land of Egypt could not read or write, so, for a small fee, a scribe would write letters and wills for them, or put down the terms of a sales agreement. Joseph loved to watch as the scribes carefully dipped their brushes in ink and began to form the letters of the Egyptian alphabet. Called hiero-glyphics, the letters looked like tiny pictures to Joseph. It amazed him that a few wiggly lines of ink could express thoughts and feelings.

One day, an older scribe noticed the young slave watching intently.

"You, come over here!" the friendly scribe called to Joseph. "I have seen you watching us every day. Can you write?"

Joseph shook his head. "No, sir. I am only a house slave. My master Potiphar uses me to run errands and to do the marketing. But tell me, those lines you just made—what do they say?"

The scribe laughed and put down his brush. "It says— 'My dearest: Your lips are like roses and your teeth are pearls. Meet me tomorrow night by the temple on the river bank.'"

"Really? Those few brushstrokes say that?"

Joseph looked doubtful.

"I see you are too sharp to fool," the scribe chuckled. "Actually, these hieroglyphics are for Pharaoh's advisors. They are a listing of all the treasures in the king's storehouse. Here, it is not hard. You try." And the scribe held out his brush to Joseph.

The young slave dropped his bundles and sat down beside the scribe. On a scrap of reed paper, he tried to copy the letter the scribe had drawn for him. When he had finished, the older man studied it critically.

"Not bad. Not bad at all. You have a good eye and a steady hand, my friend. Stop by my table whenever you can and I will give you some letters to practice."

Joseph visited the scribe every chance he got. In between market days, he would practice writing on his own. It was not long before he was writing simple words and numbers. One evening, Potiphar found his young slave sitting in the garden, scratching his letters in the sand.

"You can write?" he gasped. "How did you manage to learn?"

"I know only a few hieroglyphics, sir," Joseph

admitted. "The scribe at the marketplace lets me watch. I hope you do not mind." The youth suddenly looked worried. To give up writing now would be a shame.

"Not at all!" Potiphar exclaimed. "If you can master writing, there will be much important business you can assist me with. Let me talk to the scribe. Perhaps I can arrange for him to give you a real lesson each day. Would you like that, Joseph?"

The slave nodded. "Oh yes, sir. I would like very much to be more useful to you. Thank you, sir! You are very kind to your servant."

So Joseph grew, both in knowledge and in experience. Month by month, Potiphar gave him more responsibility. No matter what job Joseph undertook, it turned out well, for the Lord was with him. A year passed and one day, Potiphar summoned the young slave to his side.

"I am very pleased, Joseph," he said. "From this day on, you shall be my overseer. I am placing you in charge of everything that I own. No other slave in this house could I trust with such an important job."

Joseph bowed before his master. "A thousand

thanks, kind sir," he said. "But if you have found me worthy, it is only because my God has favored me with wisdom and strength."

Potiphar laughed. "Then may your God continue to favor you! It is good business for this house!"

With Joseph in charge, wealth seemed to flow into Lord Potiphar's storerooms. The officer's crops flourished and his herds of cattle grew large.

Other slaves worked diligently for the young overseer, and the great house shone with polished silver, alabaster and white linen. Dinners at Potiphar's house became famous throughout the city for the fine foods and wine that were served.

Potiphar no longer laughed at his Hebrew servant's God. Indeed, he himself came to realize that the Lord was with Joseph in a very special way. Every day, Potiphar left the king's palace knowing that Joseph would care for the estate as well as if it were his very own.

All during this time, someone else was watching Joseph closely: Potiphar's wife. From the beginning, the young Hebrew's bright eyes and strong body had attracted her. So it was one day, while her husband was away, Lady Potiphar went to

Joseph as he worked and smiled at him shyly.

"Oh, I am so lonesome today, Joseph," she sighed. "Come to my private rooms and we will sit and talk together. There is much I wish to learn about your land of Canaan."

Lady Potiphar had gone to a great deal of trouble to look attractive to Joseph. She had brushed and oiled her long black hair until it glistened in the sun. Her eyelids were outlined with dark makeup and her lips were stained a bright red. The dress she wore fit tightly, revealing her curves. Reaching for Joseph's hand, she ran her painted fingernails teasingly across his wrist.

Joseph drew back in shock. "Madam, my master Potiphar trusts me with everything he has, even you, his wife. It would be very wrong of me to go with you to your private rooms. How could I sin against God in this way?" So Joseph turned from her and quickly went to attend to his duties in another part of the large house.

But Potiphar's wife did not give up. She had played this game with many other men, and she was used to winning. Every day, after her husband left to go to Pharaoh's palace, she would stop Joseph and tease him for a kiss. She promised him great rewards if only he would fall in love with her.

"There is more than one way for a slave to earn his freedom, Joseph," she said. "Is the price I ask so unpleasant? Come, a few kisses and an afternoon together—that is all I ask. You are safe with me. Potiphar is busy all day at the palace. He will never know."

As much as Joseph desired his freedom, he knew he must not give in to Lady Potiphar's demands if he were to walk honorably with the Lord and with his master Potiphar. So Joseph did his work in the outer rooms of the house, far from the lady's chambers. But one day, she finally cornered him. The rest of the servants were working in the garden. Only she and Joseph were inside. This time, Lady Potiphar was not shy at all.

"I order you, Joseph, kiss me," she demanded. "Come into my room, now!" And she grabbed at Joseph's cloak.

The young man tore himself away and charged out of the house, leaving his cloak behind.

In that moment, Potiphar's wife realized that no matter how she tried, Joseph would never agree to love her. She began to tremble with rage. No other man had ever refused her before.

"Help! Help!" she screamed. "That awful foreign slave Joseph tried to kiss me! He wanted to humiliate me and my husband! He waited until my husband was gone and he pushed me up against the wall and tried to put his mouth on mine. Here is his cloak as proof! When I screamed, he ran away and left it behind. Help, oh help!"

The other servants came running. When they heard Lady Potiphar's story, their hearts sank. They knew Joseph too well to believe that her words were true, but that did not matter. He was a slave and she was his mistress. Besides, no matter what Joseph said to defend himself, there were no witnesses. Lady Potipar could accuse Joseph of anything she wanted to.

The slaves went and found Joseph. They tied his hands and feet with rope so he could not flee. Then everyone in the house waited nervously. What would Potiphar do when he heard? A master had the right to kill a slave who harmed his wife.

"What? Joseph did what?" At first, Potiphar could not believe the news about his most trusted servant. He turned to look over at his wife who sat crying before him. "Tell me everything," he demanded.

So Potiphar's wife began once more to tell the story she had made up. She played her part well, trembling as she described how Joseph had secretly looked at her for many days. Then her voice sank to a whisper when she told how he had touched her hand and tried to kiss her, how—

"Enough!" Potiphar roared. He was a jealous man, and his blood boiled at the thought of a slave putting his hands on his wife. No matter how valuable Joseph was, he could not go unpunished. Potiphar summoned his other servants who stood waiting outside the room.

"Take Joseph," he commanded. "Take Joseph and throw him into Pharaoh's darkest dungeon! Let him learn that the price for touching my wife is very high. Let Joseph know it will cost him the rest of his life— in prison!"

So Joseph was hustled off to jail. No one listened as he tried to explain. No one believed he was innocent. No one remembered how well he had served Master Potiphar. He was only a slave, a foreign slave accused of the unthinkable crime of touching an Egyptian noblewoman.

The huge iron door of the prison cell clanged shut and Joseph found himself face down in moldy straw. Heavy chains bit into his wrists and ankles. Bugs crept into his hair. Rats rustled in the corner, looking for scraps of food. Screams and moans of other prisoners echoed through the jail. And Joseph cried out loud.

"Lord God, save me! Do not let me spend my life rotting in this cell! Help me, O God! You alone know I did nothing wrong in Potiphar's house. Only You know I did nothing to deserve slavery. Why am I here, Lord? Why?"

Long hours passed as the young man wept and wept. At last there were no tears left. Joseph slowly sat up and gazed at the tiny patch of sunlight that streamed in through the cell window. That is when he first felt it—the presence of the Lord. Joseph's hands were still chained, his body still crawled with bugs, but he knew in a very real way that God Himself was there in the cell with him.

Memories of the dreams he had dreamed back in his father's home suddenly came flooding into Joseph's mind. "Yes, Joseph," God seemed to say that day in the prison, "I sent you those dreams, for I am your God. I know the plans I have for you, plans to give you hope and a future."

Joseph wiped his eyes and squared his shoulders. God was with him! The Lord had not forgotten him. Somehow, God would prosper him, even in prison.

Clang-clang! The jailer banged on the bars of the cell with food for the new prisoner. Joseph gratefully accepted the cup of watery porridge.

"Thank you, sir. I am Joseph, former overseer of Captain Potiphar's household. I am a good worker. Let me help you with that heavy bucket."

The jailer paused for a moment, studying the young prisoner suspiciously. But the bucket of porridge was heavy, and he was tired, and the prisoner's chains looked secure. With a shrug of his shoulders, the jailer opened the cell door and handed Joseph the bucket. Following the jailer to the next cell to serve up the porridge, Joseph rejoiced. "Thank you, O Lord," he whispered. "I will walk in Your ways all my life, even here in this place."

Joseph speaks to Pharaoh

CHAPTER 6
Dreams in the Night

"Joseph, where do you want the new prisoner to be placed?"

"Joseph, here is the grain you ordered. Should I take it to the prison cooks?"

"Joseph, this is a message from Pharaoh's palace. See that the jailer gets it when he returns."

It was not many months before Joseph was practically running the prison. From the very first day he had arrived, the young man had proven to be a trustworthy worker. First, the jailer let him deliver meals. Later, he gave Joseph permission to help with other chores. The young Hebrew swept out the cells and aired the insect-riddled mats the prisoners slept on. He emptied chamber pots and scrubbed dishes. He helped in the prison kitchen, baking bread and stirring porridge. After several months, when the jailer had learned he could trust Joseph, he would lend the young man a dull knife for a few hours. Other prisoners would line up outside Joseph's door to get long tangled hair cut off and itchy beards trimmed.

Most of the prisoners in Pharaoh's jail did not do work. Some spent the long days weeping and dreaming of their freedom. Others, who were in for life, quarreled and fought amongst themselves, or tossed the gambling stones, winning tidbits of food from their fellow prisoners and the guards.

Only Joseph worked willingly and cheerfully. He himself remained a prisoner with little hope of ever being released, but he had found useful work to do. Working kept him from falling into despair. Often, he prayed.

After a year had passed, the jailer made Joseph his chief assistant. Nothing happened inside the prison that the young man did not handle well, for the Lord was with Joseph and gave him success in all that he did. With Joseph in charge, the jailer knew he had nothing to worry about.

The months turned into years and Joseph stayed busy running the prison. But every night, resting in his cell, he thought of his father Israel and his younger brother Benjamin far away in Canaan. "The one desire of my heart, Lord," he prayed, "is to see my family again some day."

Some time later, the jailer brought two new prisoners to Joseph. Both men were dressed in fine linen and wore gold chains around their necks. Weeping and moaning, they told Joseph their sad stories. One man had worked as the royal baker; the other was Pharaoh's butler. Somehow, they had made the king angry and he had ordered them thrown into jail.

"Unless Pharaoh himself sends for us," the butler explained, "we are doomed to spend the rest of our lives in this prison."

And the men fell weeping on Joseph's shoulders. He took pity on the former court officials and tended to their needs. He helped them learn the ways of the prison. The two men found the young Hebrew to be a faithful friend, and they spent much time together. Joseph loved to hear their stories about Pharaoh, of the hard work required to manage a mighty kingdom such as Egypt. As the butler and the baker told of all that went on in the palace, Joseph would play a little game. "Hmmm," he would say to himself, "if I were ever in Pharaoh's place, how would I handle that situation?" It was a small enjoyment, locked off as he was from the outside world. Joseph found it fascinating to think of solutions for Egypt's problems.

Weeks passed, and one morning, as Joseph went in to see his friends, he noticed a worried look on each man's face. "Why are you two so downcast this morning?" he asked kindly.

"We both had dreams in the night," the baker said. "The dreams are puzzling, and there is no one to explain them to us."

Now in those days, there were wise men in the land of Egypt who were skilled in interpreting dreams. They served Pharaoh and the members of his court. Some of them sought wisdom from Re, the sun-god that the people of Egypt worshipped. Others among the wise men turned to magic and sorcery, looking for meaning in leaves floating on the Nile, or in the stomach of a butchered chicken.

Pharaoh welcomed all of them to his court. He valued wise advice, no matter where it came from. The butler and the baker, had they not been in prison, would have gone to a wise man for an interpretation of their dreams. But Joseph had another idea.

"Do not all dreams and their meanings belong to my God, the true living God? Tell me what you dreamed, and my God may reveal His wisdom to us."

The butler went first. "In my dream I saw a vine, and on the vine were three branches. Blossoms grew and clusters of grapes formed. I looked down, and Pharaoh's cup was in my hand. So I took the grapes and squeezed them into the cup and I gave it to Pharaoh to drink."

The butler scratched his chin. "Can your God tell you what this dream of mine means?"

Joseph looked thoughtful for a minute, then spoke slowly. "Here is the meaning. The three branches stand for three days. Within three days, Pharaoh will order your release from prison. Once again, you will serve him as chief butler in the palace."

Delighted with this news, the butler grabbed his friend and began to dance around the cell. Joseph put out a hand to stop him. "I have a favor to ask," he said, "in return for telling your dream. When you are back in Pharaoh's good graces, remember me, and ask the king for my freedom. Many years ago I was kidnapped from the land of the Hebrews and brought to Egypt. Here I worked as a slave, serving my master faithfully. I did nothing wrong, and do not deserve to be imprisoned."

"Dear friend," the butler promised, "you have my word of honor. For giving me this good news, I will certainly speak of you to the king! Then perhaps he will grant your release and allow you to return to your home in Canaan."

"What about me? Do not forget about me!" the baker broke in. "What does my dream mean, Joseph? Can you give me good news, too?"

Joseph listened as the baker told his dream of carrying three baskets of bread on his head. The pastries on the very top were for Pharaoh, but birds continually swooped down and ate them. This time, however, the meaning of the dream that God revealed to Joseph was not good.

"In your dream," Joseph told the baker, "once again, the three baskets stand for three days. I am sorry to tell you, my friend, that in three days' time, Pharaoh will chop off your head, and the birds will come and peck the flesh from your bones!"

The baker's face crumbled. Unlike the butler, he hoped that Joseph was wrong. So the two men waited, one with high hopes, the other with fear and trembling, to see how events would unfold. The three days seemed endless, but at last, early on the third morning, soldiers from Pharaoh's palace guard came to the prison.

"Open up!" a soldier barked at the gates. "Today is Pharaoh's birthday, and we have orders to bring both the butler and the baker to appear before him at his birthday celebration!"

Amazement filled the faces of the two men. Joseph had been right! Just as they had dreamed, they were both heading back to the palace.

A huge grin slowly spread across the butler's face, but the baker began to cry. Joseph watched soberly as the two men were led away from the prison.

"You hold their days in Your hand, Lord," he whispered after his friends. "Remember me also, my God, I pray, and rescue me soon from this prison."

Much later that same day, a procession of noisy partygoers paraded past the jail. Curious, the prisoners inside crowded close to their barred windows and peered out.

"You!" a prisoner called from inside his cell, "You out there, what is all the commotion about? Where are you heading?"

"Have you not heard?" a man in the crowd shouted back. "One of your fellow prisoners, Pharaoh's baker, is about to be executed! We are going now to watch!"

Joseph quickly spoke up. "The other prisoner who was taken to Pharaoh today, the butler, what of him?"

The man in the crowd shrugged. "Who can understand the ways of kings? The butler is now restored, returned to his place of power in the palace." And the man rushed on with the crowd, to watch the baker's execution.

Joseph sank to the floor. The interpretations God had given him were right! Even now, the butler was in the palace, serving Pharaoh his wine once more. A tiny hope flared up in Joseph's heart. Surely, the butler would remember him. Surely, he would tell Pharaoh about the Hebrew prisoner who had done nothing to deserve jail. At last, Joseph silently rejoiced, he would be free!

Tomorrow, or the next day, soldiers would come to release him. After such a long time in prison, he would be free to make his way back home to Canaan. Free! How wonderful it would be to see his father and younger brother again! And Joseph praised God for what he thought was sure to happen very soon.

But the next day came and went, and there was no word from Pharaoh's butler. A second day passed, a third, a fourth, and still no news of Joseph's release. Then a terrible sadness filled the young man's heart, and he began to pray, more earnestly than he had ever prayed before.

"God of Abraham, Isaac and Jacob! God of my father Israel! Why have you forgotten me, here in this prison? Why have you brought me so far from my home? Set me free, Lord, and let me return to my family. Have mercy on me, O God, and hear my prayer!"

Life in Pharaoh's jail returned to normal. Joseph went about his tasks inside the prison walls as cheerfully as ever, but each night his heart ached. It seemed to him that God was silent, that there were no answers to his prayers. "Why, Lord?" he cried, night after night, "Why do You leave me here? How could it be Your will that I spend the rest of my life in this prison?"

And then one night, without warning, the vivid dreams returned, the same dreams he had dreamed long ago as a boy in his father's tents. Once again, as he slept, Joseph saw clear images of bundles of grain and stars in his dreams, all bowing down before him. Each morning he awoke, puzzled over what the dreams could mean.

"I used to think that God planned for me to be a great leader, one before whom many people would bow," Joseph mused. "How I strutted before my older brothers, wearing the beautiful coat of many colors! How they would laugh to see me now, locked away in this Egyptian prison, forgotten by everyone!"

But Joseph's dreams continued night after night, and with them, his hope was reborn. Joseph did not know what his dreams meant, but he grew certain that they were indeed from God.

"I must trust in the Lord," he told himself, "and when the time is right, He will reveal the meaning of my dreams to me. He does have a plan for my life, I am sure of it!"

Two long years passed, and nothing changed for

Joseph until the night that Pharaoh himself had some very troubling dreams.

The king of Egypt woke from his sleep drenched with sweat. "Cows!" he exclaimed to the servants who attended his bedchamber. "My dream was full of cows! Seven fat ones that came up from the waters of the river to eat grass! Then seven other cows appeared. They were so thin, that their ribs showed. And as I watched, the thin cows gobbled up all of the fat ones. What a dream that was! Hmmm, the food I ate this evening must not have agreed with me."

Pharaoh took a drink from a servant who stood next to his bed, then rolled over and went back to sleep. He had not dozed long when he began to dream again. This time the king dreamed of a sturdy stalk of grain, on which there grew seven plump kernels. As he watched in his dream, seven shriveled kernels appeared and swallowed up the seven big ones.

When Pharaoh awoke early the next day, he shook his head to clear it of the scenes he had dreamed in the night. But all morning, both dreams remained fresh in his mind. At midday, he summoned the wise men of his court to come and hear about the dreams, convinced at last that they were significant. Magicians and wizards came from all corners of the huge palace to listen to the king, but no one could tell him exactly what the puzzling dreams meant.

One wise man promised he could interpret the dreams if the king made a generous offering to Re, the sun-god. Pharaoh immediately gave the priest all that he required. After a session of loud praying, the man lit a fire and burnt the offering so the smoke would carry the gifts up to the clouds where the sun-god lived. Then everyone waited for the god to give his priest the meaning to Pharaoh's dreams. After an hour of silence, the priest knew no more than he had when he started, so the king called in the next man.

Wearing a helmet in the shape of a dog's head, this wise man requested a big tray of food be brought to the throne room. Getting down on all fours, like the dog-spirit he served, the man barked and then bent his head down to eat from the tray. He claimed that eating food offered to the dog-spirit would give him the thoughts of the spirit. But it did not work.

Another man was brought in, a magician who

used a pouch of colored stones to read the future. After shaking the pouch and chanting the words of a magic spell, the man poured the stones out on the palace floor. Studying the pattern in which the stones landed, he looked for the meaning of the king's dreams. Pretty as they were, the stones shed no light on the mystery.

Still another wise man brought in armloads of scrolls. He had collected the writings of magicians from all over the world. The man spent an hour searching the scrolls for information about dreams. He read about cows and stalks of grain, but nowhere did his scrolls give him the meaning of the king's dreams.

And so it went for the entire afternoon, as man after man used all the skills at his disposal to interpret Pharoah's dreams. But no one could tell the king anything. During this time, the butler had stood faithfully by Pharaoh's side, ready to bring whatever food or drink the king might request. He had listened as the wise men struggled to interpret Pharaoh's dreams, but only when they all had failed did he remember his old friend from prison, Joseph.

"Oh, good king," the butler cried, "I have

broken a promise to a friend! I know just the man to tell Pharaoh the meaning of his dreams. He is a prisoner in Pharaoh's own jail, a Hebrew who honors his own God. When the baker and I were in jail two years ago, this man interpreted our dreams for us, and everything happened just as he said! He predicted that the baker would be executed, and three days later, Pharaoh's soldiers killed him. This prisoner told me I would return to your service, and here I stand before you to this day! I promised that I would speak of him to you, but I had forgotten until this very moment. I urge you now, O king, summon this man from prison. I am sure that he will be able to tell you the meaning of your disturbing dreams!"

The king sent for Joseph at once.

Before they left the prison, the guards helped Joseph put on a white linen skirt embroidered with golden threads. They shaved all the hair from his head except for a section that was wound into a thick braid on one side. They showed him how to bow properly when he came before the king. At last, Joseph was ready. The day he had prayed so long for had come! As he walked out the iron doors of the jail, the other prisoners clapped and cheered.

"Good-bye, Joseph! May your God bless you!"

"You have been a true friend, Joseph. I hope your freedom is long and happy!"

"Do not forget us, Joseph. Come and visit us someday when you are a wealthy man."

Even the meanest criminals in the jail were glad to see their kind, hard-working friend go free.

Pharaoh, however, eyed Joseph with suspicion.

"I had two bad dreams last night," he complained, "and none of the wise men in my court could explain them. But my butler assures me that you will be able to interpret these dreams. I ask, how can one such as you possibly know the things that my wisest advisors do not know?"

Joseph bowed so low before the king, the braid on his head touched the ground. "Great Pharaoh," he replied, "I myself cannot give you what you desire. I am only the son of a Hebrew herdsman, and I have worked in your country as a slave, first in Potiphar's house, then in Pharaoh's very own prison. But the God I serve, the One God, the God of heaven and earth, the great and living God—He is the One who will reveal the meaning of your dreams!"

"Then by all means, let us proceed!" Pharaoh said. "What items will you need to summon the spirit of your God?"

A tiny smile played around Joseph's lips. "None, honored sir. The only thing my God requires is an honest seeking heart."

Pharaoh marveled at this answer. Immediately he plunged into a description of his dreams. He told of the seven thin cows eating the seven fat ones, and how seven shriveled kernels of grain swallowed up seven plump ones. When he had finished, Pharaoh sat back in his throne, studying the simple man who stood before him.

Joseph's eyes were closed. He held his hands out, palms open to the sky. Everyone in the throne room waited silently. After only a moment, Joseph opened his eyes.

"Thank you, O God," he said quietly, then looked directly into Pharaoh's eyes. "Your two dreams are one and the same, great sir. In them, God reveals what He is about to do. The seven fat cows and the seven plump kernels of grain both stand for seven good years, when the land of Egypt will yield great harvests. The seven lean cows and the seven shriveled kernels also represent seven years, when the east wind will dry out the land. It will be a time of famine, mighty Pharaoh, when no grain will grow in the fields to feed Egypt's people."

The king started to speak, but Joseph continued calmly. "God has given to you dreams of these things, O king, because He has firmly fixed them, and they will happen soon. Let Pharaoh look for a careful, wise man and put him in charge of all the fields of Egypt. Let Pharaoh appoint assistants to help him collect grain during the seven years of plenty. And let storehouses be built to hold the grain in reserve for the seven years of famine that will come upon the land of Egypt. Otherwise, disaster will surely strike."

A gasp of amazement spread through the room. A slave, a prisoner, a foreigner had dared to tell mighty Pharaoh what to do! Members of the court waited to hear the order for the young Hebrew's execution.

Instead, Pharaoh looked thoughtful, then motioned his most trusted advisors to approach the throne.

Meanwhile, Joseph bowed low once more. With

his head still resting on the ground, he whispered a prayer: "Thank you, God, for granting me the understanding of Pharaoh's dreams. Now, Lord, I pray the king will set me free to return to my father and my brother Benjamin."

Pharaoh's officers rushed to the king's side, and they talked softly among themselves for a time. Then Pharaoh stood and addressed the entire court.

"Can we find anyone like this man, one in whom is the spirit of God?" He motioned to Joseph to approach the throne. The young Hebrew could scarcely move from astonishment.

But Pharaoh stepped down and raised Joseph to his feet. "Since God has made all this known to you, I believe there is none so wise in all my kingdom as you, Joseph. You shall be my prime minister, and all my people are to submit to your orders. Only I myself shall have more authority in governing this land."

Then Pharaoh took a huge gold ring from his finger and placed it on Joseph's. Marked with the king's own design, the ring would be proof to all who saw it that Joseph acted on Pharaoh's behalf. Next, the king dressed him in royal robes, and put a beautiful gold chain around Joseph's neck. A chariot was readied for the new prime minister's use, and the order was given that whenever Joseph rode by, the people were to kneel before him.

Pharaoh even gave Joseph a new Egyptian name: Zaphenath-Paneah, and he arranged a marriage for him with the daughter of Egypt's most powerful priest.

In this manner, the young foreigner's place was firmly established in Egypt's royal court. There was no one who could speak against him, no one who would not bow before a man so honored by Pharaoh and by God Himself. In this manner, Joseph, the shepherd boy who had been sold into slavery by his own brothers thirteen years earlier, now became the second-most powerful man in all the land of mighty Egypt.

Joseph explains God's promise.

CHAPTER 7
Famine

The seven years of plenty passed swiftly for Joseph. There was so much work to be done.

As Pharaoh's new prime minister, Joseph began traveling through all the land of Egypt. He inspected fields and supervised the construction of huge grain warehouses. During these busy days, much he had learned from his time as a slave and a prisoner helped him. Having served as Potiphar's business manager, Joseph knew how to bargain and draw up contracts and handle money wisely. From the long years running the Egyptian prison, Joseph knew how to get different kinds of people to work together.

Most important of all, as a Hebrew, Joseph knew that the God of his fathers had brought him to power in this foreign land at this very time, to serve Him by saving the grain that would feed thousands of starving people later on.

"How great is your goodness, O Lord, to me and to all people!" Joseph rejoiced in his prayers. "When my brothers sold me into slavery, You knew the plans You had for me! When I cried out in prison, You knew the famine that would occur years later! I will put my trust in You, O Lord, all the days of my life."

Because Joseph continued to love and serve the Lord, He blessed him with great success. Just as Pharaoh had dreamed, the land produced immense harvests of grain, but Joseph was able to find capable officials in each region to manage the warehouses. For seven years, grain poured in, as much, it seemed, as the sands of the sea. The managers Joseph hired were learned men, but even they could not keep accurate records, the amount was so great. The work of saving the grain went well, but Joseph had to pay very careful attention to all the details.

During one inspection visit, Joseph watched a long line of slaves delivering grain from the fields. At the door of the warehouse, the slave at the front of the line was supposed to turn in a ticket which told the warehouse manager how much grain to expect. This was to make sure that the same amount that left the field ended up at the warehouse. But Joseph saw something that concerned him. This particular manager almost never bothered to look at the numbers written on the tickets.

When Joseph investigated, he learned that his suspicions were correct. The manager was using some of the slaves to steal sacks of grain. Because no one was keeping count at the warehouse door, it was easy for a slave to slip out of line and hide a sack of grain next door in the manager's house. The manager would take the grain to the marketplace the next day and sell it, keeping the profit for himself.

Joseph was very disappointed, and took the man aside to speak privately. "Is the pay you receive as a manager not generous enough? You make more working for Pharaoh's warehouse than you could make in any other job. And do you not realize? Every sack of grain you steal today will cause some small child to go hungry when the famine years arrive."

The manager did not agree. "Oh, Joseph, there

is already so much grain, we cannot count it. Who will ever miss a sack here or there? Pharaoh certainly will never know. I suggest you do as I have done, and use this job to build your fortune."

Joseph could not let this man continue to dishonor Pharaoh's grain storage program. By the very next day, a new manager was in place. This one proved to be trustworthy. Joseph left to visit another warehouse in another city, grateful that the problem had been caught before it had caused much damage.

At home as well as in his work, God granted the young prime minister great blessing. Asenath, Joseph's beautiful wife, daughter of a powerful Egyptian priest, learned to honor the God of her kind Hebrew husband. When their first son was born, she agreed with Joseph to give the baby a Hebrew name, Manasseh, which meant forgetfulness.

Holding his small son gratefully in his arms, Joseph looked to the heavens and poured out his heart to God. "How You have eased the sadness in my heart, O Lord! With the blessing of this child, I forget all the sorrows of the past, the cruelty of my brothers against me, the years of slavery and imprisonment. Thank You for the gift of my son. You have made me forget all my troubles."

It was true. As Joseph continued in his work as a wise and powerful leader, the hardships of his past faded from his mind. He never forgot about his father and his eleven brothers back home in Canaan, but when he thought of them, it was always with love and with great longing to see them again some day.

A short time later, God blessed Joseph with a second son, Ephraim, named in honor of the Lord's fruitfulness. And again, the powerful prime minister kneeled in thanksgiving. What joy his sons brought Joseph! Carefully, he taught them to honor the Living God, the God of Abraham, Isaac, Jacob and Israel. Daily, he prayed with them for the grandfather and the uncles they had never met, who lived far away in another land. Every night, he would take his sons out to look up at the stars.

"Manasseh, Ephraim, look! How many stars do you see?"

"Oh, Papa, too many! I cannot count so high!"

"Why do we always look at the stars, Papa?"

"Because they remind us of God's promise, my boys. Long ago, God told Abraham, your great-great-grandfather, that one day our family would grow very large, with as many children as there are stars in the sky."

"But Papa, we have only us two children in our family, me and Ephraim."

Joseph chuckled. "Oh, you have many uncles and aunts and cousins! They live far away, in a place called Canaan."

"Will we ever get to see them?" young Manasseh asked.

"God is good," Joseph told his sons, "and I believe that some day, we will all get to be one big family, together again."

The seven years of plenty quickly passed, and the storehouses were filled to overflowing with grain. Everyone in the land of Egypt watched to see what would happen next. Would the seven years of hardship of which Pharaoh had dreamed come to pass, just as the seven rich years had? Would famine grip the land, as the prime minister's God had foretold?

First, the rain that watered the land stopped falling. Then the mighty Nile River began to shrink. No longer could the people count on its waters for their crops and their animals. Seedlings planted in the fields sent out long roots, searching deep in the ground for life-giving moisture. But the crops slowly withered and died, as the soil became increasingly dry. In villages and cities all over the land of Egypt, and in regions far beyond its borders, a time of harsh drought set in, when no rain fell to water the parched land.

At the first sign of food shortages, the people of Egypt panicked.

In the beginning, they relied on the small amounts of food they had stored in their homes. Then, they bought grain from other regions that had not yet felt the drought, paying very high prices. But all too soon, they went crying to Pharaoh, begging him to begin the distribution of the grain from Joseph's storehouses.

"We are hungry, Pharaoh! Our children cry and hold their bellies! We have spent much money to purchase foreign grain. Release Egypt's grain, O king, that we might have enough to eat!"

But Pharaoh had complete trust in his prime minister to handle the situation correctly. "Go to Joseph," he told the people. "Do that which he tells you to do."

Joseph listened patiently to the people's pleas, but he did not open the warehouses until the famine had spread through the entire land. He was cautious, for he knew the grain put aside would have to last for seven long years. When there was not one sack of grain left anywhere in Egypt, and none that could be bought from all the lands beyond, he finally opened the doors to the storehouses.

Crowds came from far and wide with sacks held out to receive the life-giving grain. "Great is Pharaoh, who feeds his nation!" the thankful people shouted. "And great is Pharaoh's prime minister, Joseph, who put aside grain for us in this time of great need!"

Busy managing the sales of grain, Joseph had no time to glory in the people's praise. He had not even a moment to kneel and pray until very late each night. But every day his heart filled with praise and worship of the Lord God, who in His goodness had saved the people of Egypt from starvation. And as strangers from all over the region also began to pour into the country to buy grain, Joseph wondered. Had the famine reached

Canaan? Was there enough food for his aged father and his brothers and their families? There was no way to know. Joseph could only commit them to God's safe-keeping, as he had for so many years before.

The hot dry air that had blanketed Egypt now spread up the Mediterranean coastline until it reached the land of Canaan. Grass on the rolling hills turned brown, and streams that had tumbled into pleasant valleys dried up. Every day, old Father Israel parted the door of his tent to search for signs of rain. But there was not a single cloud in the sky, just waves of heat and dust. Israel sighed and prayed. Things were very bad among the tents of his family. Without rain, they had no crops to gather. There was no grass left to graze, so their sheep were dying.

Quietly, the women had begun to cut back on the amount of food they prepared for each meal, in order to make their provisions last as long as possible.

"How long, O Lord?" Israel asked. "How long will this dry weather last? Protect my family, I pray!"

But the days passed and there was no sign of

rain. The family got by on smaller and smaller portions of food. They watched, and they waited, and they prayed. But then one night, standing in the door of his tent, Israel heard something that stirred his heart to action. It was his little granddaughter Serah, crying herself to sleep.

"Hush, child." Serah's mother spoke so softly Israel had to strain to hear. "You do not want to disturb your grandfather. He has enough on his mind with this drought. He needs his rest."

"I cannot help it, Mama." Serah's little voice trembled with tears. "I am just so hungry! Why can't we go where there is food? Why do we have to stay here?"

"Sh-sh-sh, my daughter. Grandfather Israel knows best. This is the land God has promised to us, and here we will stay until He Himself tells us to move."

Hearing these words, Israel fell to his knees. "Is now the time, Lord?" he asked. "For so long we have kept to ourselves here in these hills. Away from other peoples, we have learned to depend on You and on each other. But tell me, Lord. Is the time here at last to leave, to go to where we can find food?"

All night, Israel prayed. And when he woke, early the next morning, he knew what to do. It was not time for the family to move. God had told him to stay. But his sons could go and buy food, and bring it back, and the family would survive. Israel had heard that Egypt had plenty of grain to sell. Sighing, he took a pouch of silver from the chest that stood in the corner of his tent.

Then he went to find his sons. They were all together in the large tent where the family ate. Dishes from the meager morning meal still sat on the low table.

"Well," old Israel said gruffly, "what are you waiting for? I have heard that there is grain in Egypt. Go and buy some for us, so that we may live and not die!"

Early the next morning, all eleven brothers lined up to tell their father goodbye, sacks for carrying grain tied on the family's donkeys. The trip to Egypt would be long and hard; Israel solemnly kissed and blessed each one. Benjamin stood at the end of the line. His father cried out in dismay when he saw his youngest son ready to go.

"No, Benjamin! Do not leave me!" Israel quavered. "There are too many dangers on the way.

I fear that harm might come to you as it did to Joseph long ago. You must stay here with me." And the old man threw his arms around his tall young son and held him close.

No one argued with Israel. They all knew how much the loss of Joseph so many years ago had hurt their father. Quietly, the other brothers took Benjamin's sacks and added them to their own. They would miss his help. Bringing heavy bags of grain all the way from Egypt would be hard work. But if keeping Benjamin at home gave Israel peace of mind, the brothers were glad to obey. With a last round of farewells, they started on the long journey.

After traveling for many days, at last they reached the border of Egypt. By now, the dusty road was packed with many other foreigners who had come to buy grain. The soldiers who guarded the gates were used to dealing with the crowds. Shouting greetings in several languages, they directed different groups of travelers to interpreters who would help them make their purchases. Israel's sons were relieved. They had worried on the journey how they would communicate, since none of them spoke the Egyptian language.

They could not have known that the prime minister himself had given the order that any Hebrews coming to buy grain were to be brought directly to him.

Ever since the famine had begun, Joseph had wondered about his family. Surely, he thought, some of them would have to come and buy food. And when they did, at long last, he would have the chance to see them once again!

So when the interpreter arrived at his office with ten bearded men wearing shepherd's cloaks, Joseph recognized them at once. They looked much older. Some even had streaks of gray in their hair. But there was no mistaking: these rough men were his very own brothers Reuben and Simeon, Levi and Judah, Issachar, Zebulun, Gad, Asher, Dan and Naphtali. But Benjamin— where was Benjamin? Had his jealous older brothers treated Benjamin harshly, just as badly as they had treated him so many years ago?

The ten bowed low to the ground, in awe of the powerful man seated before them. Joseph wore elegant Egyptian clothing and necklaces of gold; he was clean-shaven and his hair was styled in the manner of a court official. Not once did the brothers think that the man before whom they bowed was Joseph. But in that instant, Joseph remembered the dream of his youth, how his brothers' bundles of grain had bent low before his. And he marveled. Ever so long ago, God had been preparing him for this moment!

"Where are you from?" Joseph asked in Egyptian.

Reuben looked up respectfully and turned to listen to the interpreter. "From Canaan," he answered in Hebrew. "We have come to buy grain."

Joseph stared at this brother, his eyes narrow with thought. Reuben had grown old. Had he grown any wiser, Joseph wondered? The prime minister decided to test his brother.

"How do I know you are not spies from an enemy nation?" he demanded. "You have come to Egypt to see how weakened we are because of the famine! Then you will go home and tell your nation to attack ours."

Reuben's face drew up in horror as the interpreter translated Joseph's words. "No! No!" he cried. "We have come only to buy food, like so many others. We are all brothers of one father, and honest men. Sir, I assure you, we are not spies!"

But Joseph would not listen. "You look like spies to me!"

Reuben grew desperate. "Sir, how can I make you understand? There are twelve of us, all sons of one man, a herdsman who lives in the land of Canaan. The youngest brother is at home with our father, and one brother lives no more."

Joseph waited for the interpreter to translate, then looked deep into Reuben's eyes. "If what you say is true, you will not object if I test the truth of your words. As surely as Pharaoh lives, you will not leave this place unless your youngest brother comes here. Send one of the others home to get him; the rest of you will be held in prison until they return. In this manner we will see if your words are true. Guards, seize these men!"

Before the brothers could sputter a protest, Egyptian guards grabbed them and shoved them roughly into a cell—in the very prison where their brother had stayed years earlier. For three days Joseph left them there, so they would know a taste of what he had endured. Then he summoned them to appear before him, along with the interpreter.

"Do as I say," Joseph spoke commandingly, "and you will live, for I honor the living God. If you are honest men, as you claim, let one of your brothers stay here in prison while the rest of you go back and take grain for your starving families. But you must bring your youngest brother to me, so that I may know the truth of your words. If you fail to do so, I will order your executions."

Shocked by this harsh sentence, the brothers turned to one another in dismay. "Surely," Gad choked, "we are being punished because of what we did to Joseph, so long ago. We saw how distressed he was when he pleaded for his life, but we would not listen. That is why this trouble has come upon us now."

Reuben paced around the room. "Back then, did I not warn you about sinning against the boy? But you would not listen! Now, all these years later, we must give an accounting for his blood."

Having understood all that his brothers said to each other in Hebrew, Joseph turned away abruptly. Tears filled his eyes. His brothers had just admitted they had done a terrible thing to him so long ago. They were upset now about having to suffer for their evil deed. But still, they had not come to feel true sorrow for their sin. Silent sobs welled up in Joseph's throat. There could be no joyful reunion yet. His brothers were not ready.

Gathering his composure, the prime minister of Egypt turned back to the men standing before him. Remembering Simeon's cruelty in pushing him into the well so long ago, Joseph ordered him bound and led away to jail. The others he released, with sacks of grain to take home and provisions for their journey.

The nine men bowed and quickly took their leave of Joseph. Although they did not like having to leave Simeon behind, they felt great relief that they were free, with enough grain to carry back to Canaan to feed their family for many months. They traveled long into the night before they stopped to make camp.

Asher was the first to discover that their troubles were not over. "Come quickly!" he called to the others. "See in my sack—the silver I paid for the grain has been returned. Here it is!"

Their hearts sank when they looked and saw that Asher was right. Trembling, they turned to face one another. "What is this," they asked, "that God has done to us?" With heavy steps, they made their way home to Father Israel. The old man greeted them eagerly until he realized that Simeon had not returned with them. He demanded to know all that had happened during their stay in Egypt.

The brothers took turns explaining.

"The prime minister spoke very harshly to us, Father," Zebulun began. "He was convinced we were spies. We kept telling him we were honest men, the sons of one father."

Dan picked up the story. "To prove we were telling the truth, we told the prime minister about Benjamin and Joseph, that Benjamin was here at home and that Joseph was dead. But still the man was not satisfied, Father. He put Simeon in jail and told us to bring Benjamin to him. Only then would he know we were telling the truth."

Old Israel groaned and held his head. Gently Reuben told him the rest of the bad news. "The man allowed us to buy grain to bring home, but as soon as we left Egypt, Asher discovered the silver he had paid had been returned to his sack. We should look in all the sacks now, Father, for I fear what God is doing."

Israel nodded, and the brothers bent over the sacks, opening each one and sifting the grain in their fingers. In just a few moments' time, each man held silver coins in his hand, the very same coins they had carried to Egypt to pay for their grain.

"Aei-i-i-i!" Old Israel clutched his beard and cried in fear. "Everything is against me! You have deprived me of my children. Joseph lives no more, and Simeon is gone. Next, you want to take Benjamin away to Egypt. Never, I tell you! I will never let my son go with you. If anything were to happen to him, I would die of sorrow! We will live on the grain you have bought, and simply pray that the famine will end soon."

"It is a wicked thing you have done!"

CHAPTER 8
Discovery in Egypt

There was no relief from the terrible famine. No matter how sparingly they ate, the day finally came when Israel's family opened the last sack of grain the brothers had brought from Egypt.

"Sisters!" Reuben's wife called to the other women working by the fire. "Go to your tents and bring out some more of the grain your husbands brought from Egypt. I have just opened Reuben's last bag."

The women at the fire exchanged worried looks. "I have none put back," one said. "We used the last of it days ago."

"Neither do I," said another. "Our sacks were the first to be opened, shortly after the men returned from Egypt."

"As were ours also. Sister, we have no grain

tucked away."

Reuben's wife looked questioningly around the circle. All heads were nodding no. All faces wore the same expression, one of worry. "Then this is it," she said slowly. "This is the very last grain with which to keep our families alive."

Two small children dashed past the fire, laughing and shouting as they ran.

"Look at them," one of the women sighed. "Today they have energy to run and play, but how will they feel tomorrow when their bellies are empty? Oh, sisters, I fear for my children. Will this terrible famine never end? How I long for the foods we used to have in such plentiful supply! What I would not give for some grapes and melons!"

"Lamb, roasting on a stick!" laughed another. "I dream of lamb, and bread, hot from the oven and dripping with honey!"

"I would be happy with a simple bowl of beans!" another of the women said. "I never thought I would miss having beans to eat."

"Yes, a bowl of beans and a chunk of cheese!"

"Sisters, that is enough!" exclaimed Reuben's wife. "We must think of today and the future, not the past. How will we make do with one sack of grain and so many mouths to feed?"

"First, we must get the men to speak to Father Israel," someone said. "If he does not agree to send them back to Egypt for more grain, there will be no choice but to prepare to die."

"In the meantime, we will water down the porridge," another wife said. "The children and our husbands already complain about the thin soup, but we must stretch it some more."

"I say, one serving per person, with no second helpings."

"For myself, I have decided to give my portion of porridge to my little ones. Zohar is so thin, and Ohad cries himself to sleep every night because he is hungry. I can live without an evening meal."

"Yes, Tilgah, we all can. So, we will do these things?" Reuben's wife looked around the circle of women. They nodded in agreement and turned to go. "But wait," she said. "We have forgotten the most important thing of all. We must pray, sisters. Pray with your husbands and your children that God will end this awful famine."

"And in the meantime," one of the younger

wives said, "pray He will miraculously stretch this grain!"

Laughing to ease their worry, the women moved off to get on with other chores. Father Israel watched them go. He knew the grain from Egypt was running low. The frightened looks on the women's faces told the whole story. After much thought, he went to the chest in the corner of his tent and pulled out another bag of coins. Then he went to see his sons.

The family's flocks were largely gone. Many of the sheep and goats had died because there was no more grass for grazing. Some had been butchered to provide meat for the family. The few that were left were tended carefully. When the drought ended, these animals would be the beginning of their new herds. With so little work to do, the men spent many hours in the large tent where the family took their meals. Here they told stories, played games, and joked with one another to keep their minds off the famine.

But when Israel walked in, the chatter stopped. All the sons waited respectfully to hear what their father had to say. He did not waste words. "It has been many months. Go back to Egypt and buy us a little more grain." Israel tossed the bag of coins into the nearest son's lap.

Judah shook his head gravely. "The prime minister solemnly warned us not to return, Father, without our younger brother. It is useless to go unless you allow Benjamin to come with us."

Israel moaned at the thought. "Why did you ever tell that man that you had another brother? Were you trying on purpose to hurt me?"

Reuben spoke up. "We were only answering his questions truthfully, Father. How were we to know that he would ask us to bring Benjamin back? But Father, if you will entrust Benjamin to my care and permit us to take him to Egypt, I promise to bring him home again to you. If I do not, I swear, you may put both of my own sons to death!"

Israel knew there was no way Reuben could really guarantee Benjamin's safety in a foreign land. "No, no," the old man said. "I simply cannot allow you to take Benjamin to Egypt. If any harm came to him, it would put this gray head of mine in the grave!"

Judah tried next. "Father, we have no choice. You must send Benjamin with us. We must go to

Egypt at once and buy grain right away so that our children can eat and live. Do you want our whole family to die of starvation? Losing our flocks is hard enough. I myself will guard Benjamin's safety. If I do not bring him back to you, I will bear the blame forever. We have wasted much precious time, and our families are hungry. Why, we could have already gone to Egypt and been back by now!"

Israel fretted for several more days, and spent much time alone in prayer. But finally, he agreed with his sons. There was only one thing to do if the family was to have food to eat. The brothers had to make the long trip back to Egypt, this time taking Benjamin with them.

"If it must be," he told his sons, sighing heavily, "then at least do this: load your sacks with the finest products of our land. Take balm and spices and myrrh, and give them to the prime minister as a gift. Take twice as much money this time, so you can pay back the amount you found in your sacks after the last trip. Surely, someone placed it there by mistake.

"And," the old man continued, his eyes welling up with tears, "take Benjamin with you. May

God Almighty grant you mercy when you appear before the prime minister, so that He will permit both Simeon and Benjamin to come home."

Having said these words, Israel buried his face in his hands and began to weep loudly.

Reuben placed his arm around his father's shoulders. "Father," he asked, concern in his voice, "how will you manage while we are gone?"

Israel shrugged. "I have done all that I know to do. I have lived with the loss of my son Joseph for many years. If I must bear the loss of two more of my sons so that our family has food to survive, then so be it."

Quickly, the brothers packed the gifts and money to buy grain, then made their way across the wilderness. As soon as Joseph learned that they had crossed the border into Egypt, he ordered them brought directly to his own house and commanded that a feast be prepared for them.

Accustomed to living in tents on the hills of Canaan, Israel's sons marveled at the luxury of the large home to which they were taken. It was made of brick and surrounded by a beautiful garden planted with palm trees and flowers. Inside, the walls were decorated with brightly colored paintings, and comfortable chairs filled the reception room. Lamps hung from hooks high on the wall to provide light for reading from the many papyrus scrolls stored on a shelf. Gameboards had been placed on low tables, so visitors could amuse themselves while they waited for the prime minister. Servants stood ready to bring anything the guests might desire. Nevertheless, the men from Canaan began to worry.

"It's a trick, my brothers!" Gad warned. "The prime minister had the silver returned to our sacks so he could accuse us of stealing when we came back to Egypt. Any minute now, he will seize us and force us to work as his slaves!"

Alarmed at this suggestion, the brothers rushed to explain what had happened to Joseph's household manager. "Good sir," they cried, "after our first trip to Egypt, we found the money we had paid for the grain returned to our sacks. Look, we have brought it back, along with more money for the grain we wish to purchase now. We assure you, sir, we are honest men!"

The manager spoke calmly. "Do not worry. Your God, the God of your fathers, placed that treasure in your sacks. Our records show that we collected your silver." Then, to reassure them, the manager brought out Simeon, whom Joseph had held in prison when the brothers returned home after their first trip to Egypt.

With tears and shouts of joy, the brothers took turns grabbing Simeon, hugging the big man until his face glowed. Next, the household manager brought the men basins of water in which to wash off the dust of the road. Shaking out their shepherd's cloaks, they made themselves ready to greet the prime minister at noon.

Joseph soon arrived. His servants rushed to help him dismount from his chariot. They brought him fresh robes to wear, and perfumed oil to rub on his hands and face. They removed his tall colorful headdress, and combed his hair into the braid that all Egyptian nobles wore. They brought clean sandals of fine leather for his feet, and stored the heavy rings and bracelets he took from his arms.

To his brothers, Joseph seemed the very picture of a high-ranking foreign dignitary. The men bowed low and presented the gifts they had brought from Canaan. Joseph's eyes widened when he saw the piles of precious myrrh, balm and spices.

"The aged father you spoke of when we last met—how is he?" Joseph asked though an interpreter. "Is he still alive?"

"Our father is alive and well, and humbly asks, honored sir, that you accept the small gifts we have brought as tokens of our esteem. We thank you for your concern about our father's well-being. He is a very old man, and has seen many troubles in his day."

"And is this your youngest brother, the one who stayed home by your father's side when last you traveled here?"

Joseph could not take his eyes off Benjamin. The sight of his younger brother's familiar face after so many years tore at Joseph's heart. But before his brothers could reply, he turned and spoke directly to Benjamin. "May God be gracious to you, my son!"

Then Joseph ran from the room.

Hidden in a private chamber, away from his brothers' puzzled eyes, Joseph gave way to the sobs that choked his throat. Weeping, he poured out thanks to the Lord. "I will praise You forever,

O God! You have never forgotten me! You have heard the cry of my heart, and allowed me to see my younger brother once more. I will give glory to You all the days of my life!"

It took Joseph nearly an hour to calm himself enough to return to his brothers. They still had no idea that the powerful Egyptian who stood before them was their own brother Joseph, whom they had betrayed so many years ago. The servants of the household helped Joseph to a head table brimming with food; they ushered the brothers to a separate table where a place was set for each of them. The brothers watched in amazement as Joseph himself directed where each of them should sit.

"You, the tall one," Joseph said through his interpreter, "sit in the first seat. And you, the one wearing the green cloak, take the second seat." And so it went until all the brothers were seated in the exact order of their ages, from oldest to youngest. How, the brothers wondered, could the prime minister know to do this?

Next, Joseph had plates of food brought from his own table and set before each man. There was broiled beef, antelope and duck, five kinds of fish, cheese, fruits and many different vegetables, along with breads, fine pastries and candy. The men from Canaan had never seen such a feast, and they watched in amazement as Joseph filled their plates. Then they noticed something strange. Each time a plate was set before Benjamin, it was piled with five times more food than theirs were. The brothers whispered among themselves. Why did the prime minister show such favor to Benjamin?

Questions also filled Joseph's head as he watched his brothers eating with such healthy appetites. When should he tell them who he was? How would they respond? Laughter broke out at the brothers' table. Grateful that Simeon was free from jail, relieved there was no trouble over the silver in their sacks, the eleven talked and joked gently with one another.

Joseph looked thoughtful. This was not the way he remembered his brothers. Had God softened their hearts over the years? Joseph decided to find out.

Calling his manager to his side, he whispered some directions. "Fill each man's sack with grain, and on the very top, place the money he has paid us. And in the sack of the youngest man, along with the coins, hide my best silver cup, the one Pharaoh gave me from his own table."

The servant hurried to do all that Joseph had commanded, and by the time the men had finished eating, the sacks of grain were filled and ready. Bidding the prime minister farewell, the brothers set out for Canaan. They had only been on the road for a short time, however, when Joseph's men caught up with them.

"Halt, strangers!" the household manager commanded. "It is a wicked thing you have done. Why have you repaid the prime minister's goodness to you with evil?"

The brothers were stunned.

"The prime minister's own silver cup is missing, the one he treasures most," the manager explained. "He sent us to stop you and to bring you back to answer for your crime."

Reuben, the eldest, spoke for the eleven men. "Sir, how can you say these things to us? We came all the way from Canaan to pay back the money we owed you. Why, then, would we steal silver or gold from your master now? Search our sacks, sir. If the cup is found in any man's sack, let him die, and as for the rest of us, we will serve as your slaves forever."

Reuben spoke with the confidence of an innocent man.

The angry manager began to calm down. "My master is too kind to enforce the death penalty, but I warn you, if we find the cup, that man shall indeed serve as a slave for the rest of his days."

Quickly, all eleven men set their sacks on the ground. Joseph's manager began with Reuben's sack and dug his hand into the bag of grain, feeling for the silver cup. It was not there. Next, he checked Simeon's sack, then Levi's, then Judah's and so on, until only Benjamin's sack was left to be examined. The man reached deep into the grain, felt around for a moment, and with a triumphant cry, pulled the silver cup out of the sack. Its polished surface shone in the sunlight.

At the sight of the cup, the brothers cried out in agony. They tore their rough cloaks into shreds and pulled at their beards until their faces were bruised and red. They begged for mercy, but the manager ignored their pleas. Instead, he tied Benjamin's hands together with a rope and marched him back toward Joseph's house. The brothers followed sorrowfully. When they arrived, the prime minister himself was waiting for them. They fell weeping at his feet.

"What is this thing you have done?" Joseph demanded. "Did you not know that a man in my position would have the power to track down a thief and punish him?"

"What can we say, sir?" Judah sobbed. "How can we prove our innocence? God Himself has shown us our guilt. It is not for the theft of the cup that we suffer, but for an evil thing we did many years ago. Sir, we are now your slaves!"

Joseph shook his head. "No, far be it from me to make all of you slaves. Only the man who was found to have the cup shall be my slave." He pointed to Benjamin. "The rest of you, go back to your aged father in peace."

Joseph's words only made the brothers weep harder. Judah explained. "Please let me speak, and do not be angry, sir. Our brother, whom you want to keep here as your slave, is our father's youngest son. Our father loves him very much. If we return home without him, our father is sure to die of a broken heart. For you see, he already has lost one son, and could not live if he were to lose this one."

Judah continued. "Please, great sir, allow me to remain here as your servant, in place of my younger brother. Let him return home, for how can I go back to my father if the boy is not with me? No! I could never do that to him! Do not let me see the misery that would come upon my father if Benjamin were not to return home!"

Joseph's heart was pounding. His breath came in short gasps. How God had changed his brothers' hearts! They were no longer the men who had treated him so cruelly years ago. Their tears and pleas for Benjamin and for their father Israel had proved it.

At last, Joseph knew, the time had come to reveal himself to his brothers. He turned to his servants and addressed them in Egyptian. "Quickly, all of you! Leave me alone with these men!"

As the servants scurried from the room, Joseph, the powerful prime minister, overseer of Egypt's grain, fell to the floor. His loud sobs filled the room and echoed down the hall. The eleven men shifted uneasily, too frightened to move.

"Brothers, can you not recognize me yet?"

Joseph cried out in Hebrew. "I am Joseph! Tell me truly, is my father Israel still alive?"

Joseph's brothers stood speechless. They were unable to answer, for they were terrified at what they heard. Joseph, the one they had sold as a slave, was alive! Joseph, the brother they had despised, now stood before them, the most powerful man in all the land of Egypt, save Pharaoh.

What punishment for that long-ago sin would he demand from them?

Brothers reunited

CHAPTER 9
New Beginnings

"Come close to me," Joseph urged his brothers, speaking still in the Hebrew language. "Come close, and see that I am Joseph, the one you sold into Egypt!"

None of the men moved. At last, gruff Simeon inched forward. He peered at the man who stood before him, studying the clean-shaven face and the dark eyes outlined with the heavy black make-up that all Egyptian nobles wore. Simeon scratched his head. Could this handsome stranger possibly be his younger brother Joseph? So many years had passed.

Seeing Simeon's hesitation, Joseph took a towel and wiped the cosmetic from around his eyes. Then he spotted a table in the room, covered with a cloth woven in colorful stripes. The prime minister seized the covering and whirled it around his shoulders. When he lifted it to cover his head in the style of a Hebrew cloak, Simeon's eyes immediately widened.

"My brothers!" the older man gasped. "Look, truly it is Joseph! I could not recognize him until he drew the cloth around his head. Look, do you not see? It is Joseph, grown older, lacking the beard of manhood, but still wearing the coat of many colors our father gave him! Oh, Joseph! Joseph! How evilly I treated you!"

And Simeon burst into tears.

Joseph rushed to put his arm around the big man as Simeon sobbed and tried to talk. "Those months I spent in prison here in Egypt, I— I had so much time to think. All the wrong things I have done, my bad attitude, my temper—it seemed as if God Himself was speaking to me. Oh, Joseph, I am so sorry for what I did to you so many years ago!"

Simeon got down on his knees before his younger brother. "I repent of my great sin, and I ask both you and the Lord to forgive me. Joseph, do you think you will ever find it in your heart to love me as your brother again?"

Before Joseph could answer, the other brothers came and also bent down before him. Reuben spoke for them all.

"Yes, Joseph, we too seek forgiveness. We are truly sorry for how you and Father have suffered all these years because of our actions. Never did you deserve the treatment we gave you. Now the Lord has set you over us. We deserve whatever punishment you wish to give us."

Then Reuben and the others joined Simeon in his tears.

Joseph's face was wet as well, but it was with tears of joy. "My brothers! Be not distressed, any of you! Do not be angry with yourselves for selling me into slavery. Why, I forgave you long ago! Don't you see? God brought me to Egypt for a special purpose, to save many lives, my brothers, your lives! God put me to work here so that when the time of famine came, there would be food for your children, so our family would live and become a great nation, just as the Lord promised Abraham."

Joseph began to laugh through his tears. "How I rejoice in this day that the Lord has given us! Only He could bring us through slavery and famine and hardship to be together once more as brothers on this day!"

"Look around you," Joseph waved at the fine furnishings in the reception room. "God not only brought me to Egypt for a purpose, but He prospered me here as well. I am Pharaoh's overseer and enjoy many blessings. But there can be no greater blessing than seeing you, my own dear brothers, once again. How good God is, to answer my prayers!"

Having said these things, Joseph turned and threw his arms around Benjamin. He wept and wept, crying as if his tears could wash away all the years they had been apart. Benjamin also broke down and sobbed. Never had he dreamed the beloved older brother he had mourned as dead for so long was alive and well, and serving as the prime minister of Egypt!

The sound of the brothers' joyful reunion filled the halls of Joseph's home. Servants ran to the palace to tell Pharaoh what had happened, that Joseph's own brothers had come to him at last from the land of Canaan. The king was amazed to learn that these brothers were the very scoundrels who had sold Joseph into slavery. He was more amazed to hear that Joseph had received them with love and forgiveness. The prime minister could have ordered them all put to death in an instant! But Joseph, as Pharaoh well knew, was a man of exceptional character.

The king called for a messenger. "Go to Joseph's house," he commanded. "Tell my prime minister how happy I am that he has found his family after all these years. Extend to Joseph's brothers this formal invitation: to come and live here with Joseph in Egypt. Tell them to bring their father, their wives and children and all their flocks. In honor of Joseph's great service to our nation, I will offer his family the region of Goshen, the most fertile land in all of Egypt. Go quickly!" Pharaoh urged the messenger. "Take these words to Joseph and his brothers."

When Joseph received the king's message, he rejoiced. "You must go back to Canaan at once," he told his brothers, "because there are still five years of famine to come. If you remain at home, you and your children will surely die of starvation. Go and tell my father that I am alive! Tell him of the honors Pharaoh has heaped upon me here, and that I can provide for his children, his grandchildren and his flocks. Here in safety, God will preserve our family, to become a great nation which will endure for all generations."

"Oh, let us hurry, brothers," Joseph cried. "We will begin preparations for your journey back to Canaan at once. You shall stay here with me in my house until all is ready. Then you must make haste, for I long to see my father while he still lives!"

So the shepherd sons of Israel stayed in the prime minister's fine home until all was ready for their return to Canaan. The rough men found much in Egypt at which to marvel, from the great wealth of their own brother, to the ways and customs that were so different from their own. Upon waking in Joseph's soft beds the first morning, each man found Egyptian-style clothing waiting for him. The brothers made quite a sight as they struggled into the strange garments.

"Issachar, is that you? Ho-ho! That linen robe is dazzling, but is it possible you have it on backwards?" Judah asked. "I do not remember seeing the men of Egypt dressed exactly like— that!"

"I see nothing wrong with my garment, brother," Issachar snapped back. "You would be wise to check what you just tied on your head. It is supposed to be a sandal, not a hat."

"Dan, Dan, what do you think?" Naphtali whispered. "Is this a wig, or a scarf that goes across your chest?"

"Neither. I'd say it's a fancy money pouch to carry," Dan replied.

"No, no, you both are wrong," Zebulun insisted. "Even a child could see it's one of those belts the nobles wear around their waists!"

With assistance— and laughter— from Joseph's servants, all eleven men finally got their new clothing properly arranged. But they roared in protest when an attendant brought out the pots of makeup that the nobles of Egypt always wore.

"Brothers, I do not wish to offend Joseph, but I would rather die than put that smelly woman-stuff on my face," Asher exclaimed.

Joseph heard the commotion and came to explain. "Men and women alike paint their faces here in Egypt. The sun is much stronger than it is in Canaan, so the cosmetic protects them from the strong rays."

But the brothers were not convinced. They wore the soft Egyptian robes and sandals with pleasure, but refused to try the eye paint. After a time, all was in order for the trip back to Canaan.

Joseph gave his brothers sturdy wagons in which to bring all their belongings to Egypt. He provided supplies for their journey and more new clothes. And to Benjamin, son of Rachel, and his full flesh and blood, Joseph gave five sets of new clothes and three hundred pieces of silver.

The brothers also took with them lavish gifts for Joseph's father and the family. Ten donkeys loaded with the best things of Egypt stood ready to start for Canaan, along with ten more donkeys carrying grain and bread and other foods for Israel's large family.

The day for their departure came. All in Joseph's household and many from Pharaoh's palace lined the road to bid the brothers a safe journey. After hugging each man tightly to his chest, Joseph lifted his hands toward Heaven and prayed. "May the Lord watch over you and give you peace until He brings you back to me once again."

"Farewell, dear ones," he called as the brothers led the donkeys and wagons down the road. Then his last words made everyone laugh: "And brothers, please, for my sake, try not to quarrel amongst yourselves on the way!"

So Joseph's brothers left Egypt and headed back toward the hills of Canaan. All the way home, the men talked of their father's great joy once he would hear the news that Joseph lived. Arriving at last at their father's tents, the brothers nearly stumbled over each other to stand before ancient Israel.

"Father, Father, such news!" they cried. "Your son Joseph is alive! He is overseer of all the grain in Egypt, second only to Pharaoh himself!"

The old man stood as still as a statue, his mind unable to grasp what his sons were saying. Asher leaned close and spoke clearly in his father's ear. "Joseph is alive! Look, these fine things are his gifts to you!" And Asher pointed to the wagons and donkeys they had brought from Egypt.

Israel frowned. He squinted at the wagonloads of food and supplies. He looked back at his sons to see if they were trying to trick him. But the joy shining in their eyes convinced him.

"It must be true!" the old man gasped. "Your faces could not look as they do if you were lying. God in Heaven, Joseph is alive! My son Joseph lives!" Overcome with emotion, Israel staggered.

His sons reached out to keep him from falling. But the old man recovered quickly. "Bring my traveling cloak at once," he commanded. "I must go to see my son before I die."

"Not so fast, Father," his sons laughed. "We must unload Joseph's gifts before we can pack up to leave!"

The family crowded around the wagons, eager to see the things Joseph had sent from Egypt. He had thought of everything.

For his brothers, he had packed razor-sharp knives and tools, made by Egyptian craftsmen from the finest iron. There were wineskins filled with delicious date and palm wines, so the men could refresh themselves on the long journey back.

The women were thrilled to discover the polished mirrors and shell combs that Joseph had sent them. Dipping their fingers into vials of fragrant Egyptian perfume, they massaged it into their skin and studied their reflections. For more practical purposes, Joseph included clay storage pots painted with colorful Egyptian designs.

Even the children received gifts from Egypt. There were spinning tops and marbles, stuffed leather balls and dolls carved from wood. Little granddaughter Serah was delighted when she opened what she thought was a sewing basket, only to find a tiny kitten curled up inside. Everyone stopped to watch as the furry creature yawned and stretched, then rubbed up against her new mistress. It was the first cat any of them had ever seen.

But the best gift of all was the one Joseph sent for his father Israel. It was a magnificent leopard skin he had purchased from an African trader who had come to Egypt for grain. The family crowded around to feel the silky fur and to marvel at its richly colored spots. His sons helped Israel drape the skin around his shoulders.

"Look everyone!" Zebulun called. "Our father looks like a royal chief!"

The old man strutted around, enjoying all the attention.

"You will have to save your fine skin to wear when Joseph takes you to meet Pharaoh, Grandfather," one of the older boys suggested.

"Nonsense," Israel replied. "I am going to wrap up in it every night. This fur is just the thing I need to keep my old body warm! But let us put our gifts aside for now and get ready to go. I need to see my Joseph!"

Despite Israel's impatience to leave, it took the large family several days to pack up their new gifts and their old belongings and prepare for the long trip to Egypt. There were cooking pots to scrub, and tools to clean and sharpen. Tents were mended, new sandals were cut from tough leather, and cloaks were patched to keep out the sun and the wind. With so many children and animals, the family's trip would be a slow one. But at last, they pulled up their tent stakes and headed for Egypt.

Old Israel battled with his emotions. Each step down the road that took him closer to Joseph also brought him out from the land of his fathers. The old man knew he would never set eyes on the beloved hills of Canaan again. Each stream, each bend in the path, each grove of trees brought memories to his mind.

Here was where he had played as a boy beside Esau his brother. . . .

Here was the place he had dreamed as a young man of the staircase to Heaven. . . .

Here was the spot where his grandfather Abraham had buried his beloved wife Sarah. . . .

Israel grieved as he bid a silent farewell to his homeland. He was grateful that his family would escape the famine by living with Joseph in Egypt, but he knew in his heart he would always long for Canaan.

A short time later, Reuben called back from the front of the line. "Father, look! Beer-sheba is just ahead! It is the last place to water the flocks before we leave Canaan. Should we stop?"

Israel did not have to think twice. Certainly they would stop at Beer-sheba. It had been the home, years ago, of Abraham and Isaac. Israel would be glad to linger there once more before crossing the desert into Egypt.

The first thing he did after his sons helped him down from the wagon was to set up an altar of stones. "We must make an offering," he told them. "We have so much for which to give thanks. God has blessed us for three generations in Canaan, and we must ask Him to go with us now into a strange land, to Egypt, where we will see Joseph once more." Israel's sons and daughters, his grandchildren and all his attendants offered prayers and gifts to the Lord at Beer-sheba.

That night, as Israel slept, God spoke to him in a vision. "Israel, Israel!" a mighty voice called out. "I am God, the God of your fathers. Do not be afraid to go down to Egypt, for I will make your children into a great nation there. I will be by your side as you go, and I will surely bring you back to this land again one day."

Israel awoke to find new strength and courage flowing through his aged body. He marched into the desert with a sure step, confident that God would help him in the strange new land toward which they traveled.

His family that day numbered sixty-six men and boys, along with their wives and numerous daughters. There was Jemuel and Carmi, Tola and Shuni, Heber and Ashbel. There was little Malchiel and granddaughter Serah, Imnah and Elon and Shimron, all talking at once, all pushing and shoving. Israel chuckled as he studied the large noisy family streaming down the road. "You promised Abraham descendants as numerous as the stars. Lord, couldn't You make them as silent as the stars as well?"

When they had crossed the desert and reached the border of Egypt, Israel sent Judah on ahead, to meet Joseph and to get directions to Goshen, the fertile land Pharaoh had offered to them. Joseph had been waiting for days, and when he saw his brother Judah coming, he leaped into his chariot and rode out swiftly to meet him. The two journeyed to Goshen together, and it was there, after so many years of separation, that Joseph and Israel embraced each other at last.

Father and son wept together for a long while, but finally Israel straightened up to study Joseph's face. There, he seemed to read all the suffering and loneliness Joseph had known, as well as the wisdom and power and blessing he had gained in the land of Egypt. The father liked very much what he saw in his son.

"Now let me die," he told Joseph, "for I have seen you with my own eyes and I know for a certainty that you walk with the Lord."

Joseph gave the wrinkled old man a tender look. "You cannot die yet, Father. I need to be with you, and besides, we must go pay our respects to Pharaoh, to assure that he will continue to grant the land of Goshen to our family." So Joseph, his father, and five of the brothers went to call on the king.

Although Israel and his sons were wealthy men in Canaan, never had they even dreamed of the splendor they now saw in the Egyptian palace. Gold lined the walls and cool marble tiles laid out in lovely patterns formed the floors on which they walked. Tall columns painted with colorful designs towered overhead. Pharaoh himself sat on a throne carved from dark wood and studded with precious stones. Great gold wings spread across the back of the chair. They were the wings of the sun-god Re.

"Honored Pharaoh," Joseph said, bowing low before the throne, "my father and my brothers have arrived from Canaan. They have brought their flocks and all their possessions. With your permission, sir, they wish to settle in the land of Goshen as you yourself proclaimed." Joseph motioned to his five brothers and they, too, bowed before the powerful king of Egypt.

Pharaoh studied the strong Hebrew men.

"What is your occupation?" he asked them.

"Great sir, we are shepherds, as our fathers were before us. We have come to live in Egypt, as Pharaoh well knows, because there is no grass left anywhere in Canaan on which our flocks may graze. We request leave, sir, to live in Goshen."

Pharaoh was glad to grant the request. There was a great need in Egypt for capable shepherds. "Goshen will be the best place for your brothers," the king told Joseph. "Now, Joseph, I want to meet your aged father."

When Israel came to stand before the king, he bowed, and then lifted his hands high to Heaven. In a strong clear voice, Israel prayed that his God, the living God, the one true God, would shower Pharaoh with many blessings. Joseph's brothers watched nervously. The Egyptian king did not honor the Lord; he served idols made of silver and gold. Would Israel's prayer offend him?

But Pharaoh saw only an honorable old man, who had raised a remarkable son. Kindly, the king asked, "Elderly sir, how old are you?"

"A hundred and thirty years, O king. My years have been many and difficult, but the Lord has blessed me greatly." Israel bowed once more and went out from Pharaoh's presence.

Joseph rejoiced. The meeting with the king had gone well. Goshen would be a safe and secure home for his family during the years of famine that remained.

A message from Pharaoh

CHAPTER 10
Good Times in Egypt

Goshen was a sight for sore eyes!

Israel nodded approvingly as the wagons pulled to a stop on the crest of a hill. Spread out in all directions, for as far as the eye could see, were green grazing lands.

"Lord, O Lord," the old man whispered worshipfully, "Your goodness to me is exceedingly great. Everywhere we have traveled, through Canaan and here to Egypt, there has been only parched land and death. But You, O Lord, have led us to life and green pastures once more. We shall praise Your name forever!"

Israel looked over at Joseph, seated next to him in the wagon. The father's eyes filled with tears of love and gratitude. Many times over the last few days, Israel had marveled at all God had done through this son of his. In long years of hardship in a foreign land, God had kept Joseph faithful. He had given him wisdom, and that blessing had saved all of Egypt as well as his own family from starvation. And now, God had rewarded him, bringing the whole family together once again in a place of safety. Joseph was right. Goshen was the perfect spot for his family to rebuild their flocks and to live in peace and plenty for as long as the famine raged.

There was another reason Father Israel liked Goshen. Very few Egyptians lived there. Most of them preferred city life. Here, in the lonely Egyptian grasslands, it would not be hard for his children to continue living as devout Hebrews. If they had settled closer to the crowded Egyptian cities, they would have seen altars to pagan gods on every street corner. Israel knew that his family's survival depended on their relationship with the Lord. His heartfelt prayer was that, even in pagan Egypt, his children would always serve the God of their fathers.

"Father, what do you think of Pharaoh's gift to us?" Joseph asked. "Shall we look for a suitable place to set up the tents?"

Father and son eagerly got down from their wagon and began to study the land before them. They were soon joined by the other brothers, as well as some of the women and all of the children who were old enough to tumble and play in the soft green grass. Everyone was excited about the family's new home.

It was not long before a campsite was selected. With much laughing and talking and debating, the wagons were pulled into place. Then the busy work of unloading and settling in began. Joseph worked alongside his brothers, helping to pitch the family's large tents, unpacking chests and baskets, sweating in the hot sun. No one back in Pharaoh's palace would have recognized Egypt's famous prime minister.

Joseph stayed in Goshen for several weeks. For the 32-year old man, it felt as if he were a young boy again. During the day, he staked out new pastures and tended the sheep. At the evening meal, he sat at his father's right hand, with his brothers on either side, glowing in the warmth of their love. Nights he spent in Benjamin's tent, just as he had done in his boyhood, even though he and Benjamin were both grown, with wives and children of their own. Everyone agreed: it was a sweet time of blessing for the whole family.

But the day finally came when Joseph had to leave. A swift chariot rode into Goshen with a message from the king. The famine in Egypt continued, and the prime minister was sorely needed to oversee the fair distribution of food. With tears in his eyes, Joseph embraced each member of his large family, from old Father Israel down to the tiny baby Benjamin's wife held in her arms. He promised to return whenever he could, and to bring his own small sons with him. The brothers walked by Joseph's side until they reached the last hill of Goshen.

"Take care, Joseph," Naphtali said. "We will pray God's wisdom for you as you serve Pharaoh."

"And do not worry about Father. We will always honor and care for him," Asher added.

"Many thanks for all your provisions, and for bringing us here," Reuben said, giving Joseph a grateful hug. "Our children will live because of you!"

One by one, each brother said a last goodbye. Finally it was Simeon's turn. He spoke softly, with downcast eyes.

"That you could forgive us, Joseph, after all the evil we did to you— it still amazes me! We do not deserve a brother as good and kind as you."

Joseph reached out to hug the big man. "The Lord treats us as we deserve, Simeon. Let us always remember, and serve Him with gladness!"

A bargain for grain

CHAPTER 11
The Wise Ruler

The third year of the famine was just beginning, and thanks to Joseph, the storehouses still had plenty of grain to sell. There was only one problem: the people had no money left with which to pay for it.

"Give us the grain, Joseph," they cried. "We have no money left! We spent all we had buying grain from Pharaoh's storehouses last year and the year before that. Now our money is all gone, but the famine continues, and we do not want to die of hunger. So we beg you, give us the grain!"

But Joseph was very wise. He saw an opportunity to strengthen Pharaoh's power. He told the people, "I know your money is all gone, and that you and your children are hungry. But Pharaoh is kind. He will not let you starve. He will give you grain in exchange for your livestock. Bring the animals to his store-houses, and then you will receive the food you need."

In this manner, Joseph increased Pharaoh's herds. By the end of the year, the king owned all the horses, sheep, goats, cattle and donkeys in the land of Egypt. And the people were grateful that they and their children had food to eat.

During the fourth and fifth years of the famine, Egypt's farmers came to Joseph. They were very worried. "Sir," they said, "we cannot hide the fact that our money and all of our livestock is gone. We have nothing left with which to purchase food except for our farmland. Prime Minister Joseph, please let us trade land for food, so that our children might live."

Once again, Joseph proved to be a good manager for his king. He bought all the land that the Egyptians owned, giving the people grain to eat in exchange for their property. Pharaoh's government increased in strength and power. And the people continued to give thanks for Pharaoh and his prime minister.

"Starvation!" they cried, "starvation and death would have been our lot if Pharaoh had not set

Joseph over Egypt's grain."

Drought had such a strong hold on the land that the people talked of little else. Every morning, their first thoughts were of rain. Farmers rushed from their beds to study the sky. Priests prayed that Egypt's gods would fill the clouds overhead with moisture. There was nothing left in all the land and even in distant regions that was not dry and shriveled up. Even the mighty Nile River had dwindled down to a mere trickle of water in a bed of sun-cracked mud.

"Surely," people said, "the time for change is here. We have had five years of this terrible dryness. Any day now, the weather will change. It just cannot continue like this much longer."

But Joseph knew better. He trusted in the dreams that God had given Pharaoh. He knew there were still two years of famine left.

The sixth year came, and then the seventh, with no signs of rain to be seen. The people continued to come to Pharaoh's warehouses for grain, but they had absolutely nothing left with which to pay. Their money, their livestock and their land had all gone into Pharaoh's treasury. In desperation, the hungry people finally cried, "Buy us,

Joseph! We have nothing left to trade but our bodies. Give us grain to eat, and we will gladly serve as Pharaoh's slaves!"

Joseph did as they asked, putting down each man's name on a list. Then the people took their portions of grain and went home and ate. The seven years of famine had cost them everything—their savings, their animals, their land, even their very freedom, but the Egyptians were just glad to be alive.

Then one day, without warning, the rain began to fall. The parched earth soaked up the cooling drops like a sponge. It rained all day. Gradually, the Nile crept back toward its banks. By the next morning, the fields of Egypt were already starting to turn green. People stood with their arms outstretched, faces to the sky, rejoicing as raindrops splattered their bodies.

"Look," they cried, "the drought is ending! At long last, we can plant seed. With pleasure we will plow our fields, and they will yield us rich harvests!"

But even as the Egyptians spoke these words, their faces fell, for they suddenly remembered. They had no grain to plant; only Pharaoh had grain. They had no cattle or oxen to yoke to the plow; only Pharaoh had livestock. They no longer owned any farmland; all the fields now belonged to the king. What work they could do with their own hands was not even theirs. As Pharaoh's slaves, their work from then on would benefit his treasury. What should have been a day of rejoicing was instead very sad.

Once again, Joseph proved himself to be a leader of great wisdom. He issued a proclamation and ordered it read in every town and village throughout the land.

"People of Egypt," the proclamation read, "during the seven years of famine, you sold yourselves and all your land to Pharaoh in exchange for food. Now gracious Pharaoh wishes to make you a gift. Accept this seed from the storehouse of the king. Go home and plant it, so that the fields of Egypt may once more bring forth rich harvests, so that all the children of Egypt once more may grow prosperous. Mighty Pharaoh asks only one thing in return: that when your crop comes in each year, you give a fifth of it to him in remembrance of what he has done for you this day. The remaining four-fifths you may keep as your own, to provide seed for your fields, and food for your children from this day forth."

The Egyptians were stunned by this generous gift. They cheered their king whenever he rode through the streets in his chariot. "You have saved our lives," they cried, "and returned to us a means by which we can live. May we ever find favor with Pharaoh. We are in your debt forever!"

So Joseph's proclamation became law, that a fifth of every harvest belonged to the king. The people paid this tax gladly, because they always remembered that, by rights, they should have served as slaves. The government of Egypt had become firmly established, and for as long as Joseph served as his advisor, Pharaoh ruled wisely and fairly.

Joseph's work, however, did not lessen with the end of the famine. The king relied on the wisdom of his prime minister in many matters. There were new laws to write and enforce, and difficult judgments to make. There were building projects to plan and massive irrigation systems to maintain. Joseph's presence was required whenever rulers from other countries visited the Egyptian king. But in each and every task, Joseph served the Lord first. So God gave him success in all that he undertook.

During these busy years, Joseph only had time for brief visits with his family in Goshen. His servants would drive him out in his royal chariot so he could spend the day with his father and his brothers. What an odd sight it was— the jeweled and perfumed palace official sitting with the rough Hebrew shepherds. But all too soon the business of running Egypt would pull Joseph back to Pharaoh's palace. He began to long for the time when he could stay in Goshen forever.

"What do you think, brothers? Is there room enough to set up another tent? I will need a place to live when Pharaoh gets tired of letting me handle his problems. I could always move out here— maybe I can become the prime minister of Goshen and write laws and proclamations for all of you to follow!"

Joseph's words gave his family a good laugh.

Israel blesses Manasseh and Ephraim.

CHAPTER 12
For All Generations

There was a knock on the door of Joseph's office in the palace. "Urgent news, sir!" a voice called.

"Come in," the prime minister sighed. What was it now, Joseph wondered: a shortage of bricks for Pharaoh's latest building project, an irrigation ditch in need of repair? The now middle-aged Joseph put down the scroll he had been reading. It joined the large pile of clay tablets and sheets of papyrus that covered the entire top of the desk.

One of Pharaoh's palace guards entered the room and saluted. "There is a message from Goshen for you, sir."

At the word Goshen, Joseph's forehead wrinkled. He looked sharply at the soldier standing before him. "Yes? Is it my father? Is something wrong?"

"No, sir. Not that I know of, sir. But he asks that you come to him right away, sir. He has something important that he wishes to discuss with you."

Joseph rose immediately from his gilded chair. "Quick, have my chariot readied. We will leave for Goshen within the hour!"

As the soldier turned and stepped from the room, Joseph sank back in his seat and buried his face in his hands. Never before, in all the seventeen years they had lived in the land of Egypt, had old Israel summoned him to his side in this manner.

"O Lord," Joseph prayed silently, "is my father dying? Preserve him until I can get out to Goshen, to see him once more before he leaves this earth!"

A short time later, the prime minister's chariot raced out of the city. At Joseph's bidding, the driver touched the horses' backs with his whip. It was important that they reach Goshen as soon as possible.

"My son, my Joseph!" Old Israel's face lit up with pleasure. He stood in the door of his tent, his feeble body supported by a sturdy staff. Joseph leaped from the chariot and rushed to embrace him.

"How are you, Father? I came as soon as I received word." Joseph spoke tenderly. "Your message concerned me. Are you feeling well?"

"Of course not!" Israel chuckled. "I am nearly 147 years old! My body is tired, and I am ready to go to be with the Lord. But I do not think He is calling me home quite yet. There's still some life left in these old bones!"

The old man playfully nudged his son with his sharp elbow, and grinned.

"But the time is not far off, my son," he added in a more serious tone. "That is why I asked you to come out here today. I have some concerns about this family, about what will happen after I am dead."

Father and son turned to sit on the soft carpets that lined Israel's tent. Gently, Joseph helped the elderly man down to the floor.

"Father, do not have a care for the future," Joseph said. "Pharaoh is well-pleased to have the family stay here in Goshen. As long as I have a place in his court, we will have a home."

"But Egypt is not my home, son. It is not the home promised to me by the Lord God," Israel said. "Swear to me, with your most solemn promise, that you and your brothers will honor my last request. It is this: to be buried in the land of my fathers. Do not bury me here in this foreign land. When I die, carry me out of Egypt and bury me with Abraham and Isaac in Canaan. Will you swear to do this?"

Joseph swore. Satisfied, his father leaned back to rest in a pile of plump cushions. The old man's breathing was shallow and weak, but he cleared his throat and continued.

"There is something else, Joseph. I must know how things stand between you and your brothers. Thanks to you, we have lived here in comfort for seventeen years. My sons and their wives have had many healthy children. Our flocks have multiplied as never before. Truly, the Lord is blessing us because of your faithfulness to Him. And you, Joseph, you faithfully visit whenever your work permits. I watch as you laugh and joke with your brothers. But I must know your heart before I die. Are you still one of us, my son? Or do you crave the splendor of Egypt?"

Israel's questions struck at Joseph's very heart. He took his father's hand and looked him earnestly in the eye. "From the days of my youth," Joseph declared, "I have honored no other god but the one true living God. And I will always be the son of Abraham, Isaac and Israel— forever!"

The old man studied his son's face for a long moment. "Then there are two things you must do, Joseph. First, bring your sons, Manasseh and Ephraim, out to Goshen, that I may greet them and give them my blessing. Then, put your brothers' fears to rest. They are in awe of your wealth and your power in Egypt. They worry that someday you will punish them for what they did to you so long ago."

The old man breathed a deep sigh. "If you will do those things, Joseph, then I will go to my final resting place in peace."

At that moment, the sound of male voices came from just outside Israel's tent. Joseph quickly reached over to clasp his father's hand and then went to join his brothers. The old man watched with approval, then lifted his hands in prayer.

"I am a most happy man, O Lord, for You have saved all my sons and allowed me to see them together in one place again. Prepare Joseph for the day that I am no longer here. Give him the love and wisdom to lead his brothers wisely. And remember your promise to Abraham, to Isaac, and to me, Lord. Multiply this family, that our children will be like the stars, a blessing to all generations."

It was not long after that day that Joseph received a second message from Goshen. This one was from his brothers. Israel was dying. Once again, Joseph rushed out to the country. This time he took his sons, Manasseh and Ephraim.

When Israel heard that Joseph and his sons had arrived, he gathered the last of his strength to sit up in his bed. Squinting from eyes that were half-blind, he asked, "Are these your two boys, Joseph? Bring them closer, that I might embrace them."

The old man put out his shaky hand to feel the curly hair and firm young skin of Joseph's sons. "Fine young men. . ." he panted. "God has truly blessed us in our children."

Then Joseph and his sons knelt down by Israel's bed to receive his final blessing.

"May God, the God of my fathers Abraham and Isaac, the God who has been my Shepherd all the days of my life, wonderfully bless you, my children," Israel said. "He is the Angel who has protected me from harm. May these sons be an honor to my name and to the names of Abraham and Isaac. And, lastly, Father, may they increase greatly upon the earth, until they become a mighty nation."

The old man sank back into his bed, exhausted. Joseph struggled to hold back his tears.

"Go, Joseph," Israel managed to mutter. "Go and get your brothers. I want all of you here."

So the twelve men gathered around their father's bed. He blessed each one in turn, speaking of the good deeds they would do in the future, warning them to watch out for their weaknesses. "And Joseph is your fruitful vine. Cling to him, my sons, and to the Great Shepherd, the Almighty from whom all blessings flow."

Israel took one last breath, and died.

No one moved for a time. All the sons wept quietly, praising the Lord for their father. Joseph threw himself on Israel's body and kissed him. At last he straightened up.

"I made our father a promise, not long ago," he told his brothers, "that we would bury him in Canaan, the land of our forefathers. Let us first go to Egypt. There I will order the royal physicians to embalm our father's body so that we may make the journey back to Canaan."

It took forty days to embalm Israel's body. Pharaoh's physicians took as much care as they would had Israel been a member of the king's own family. In addition, Pharaoh declared that for seventy days, the entire nation of Egypt would mourn Israel's death. It was a sign of the great respect and gratitude the people felt for their prime minister.

But at last the time to leave for Canaan was at hand. Joseph went before Pharaoh. "Great sir," he said. "Permit me to honor my father's last request, that his body be returned to Canaan, the land of our fathers. When I have buried him there, O king, I will return to your service."

Pharaoh gladly gave his permission. So Joseph and his brothers left Egypt, carrying their father's coffin. To their great amazement, a large number of Egyptians traveled with them. Most of the king's advisors went, along with soldiers from the palace guard and members of Joseph's household staff. Many in the large crowd were just ordinary citizens, but they remembered with gratitude how the prime minster had fed their families during the famine. Everyone wanted to show sympathy and respect to Joseph's family.

Chariots, wagons, soldiers on horseback and common folk on foot went with Israel's sons all the way to Canaan. They crossed the Jordan River and there the Egyptians held a solemn funeral, followed by seven more days of mourning. Then Joseph and his brothers went on alone, to the cave of Machpelah, the cave Abraham had purchased from the Canaanites many years before. There they buried their father just as they had promised, placing his body near the spot where Abraham had buried his beloved wife Sarah.

Afterwards they all returned to their children in Egypt. That was when Naphtali finally spoke on behalf of all the brothers.

"Joseph, there is something we need to say to you. For a long time, we have known that Father would make you the head of this family, and that is right and good. But now that he is dead, you can do with us as you please. The mighty army of Egypt is at your command. If you want to, you can punish us for the evil we did to you in the past. But know this, Joseph. Before he died, Father told us to ask once again for your forgiveness, to tell you again how sorry we are that we ever sold you into slavery."

Then all eleven brothers knelt down before Joseph, tears streaming from their eyes. Asher spoke next. "We come today to beg you, brother, to forgive us. Because of us, you became a slave. Now, Joseph, we will be your slaves!"

Joseph was overcome with emotion. After all these years together in Egypt, his brothers still worried that he had not forgiven them! Joseph hurried to assure them, and his words rang in their hearts ever after: "Do not be afraid! I am your brother who loves you, not your slave master. God alone judges and punishes evil. He alone can use evil for His good purposes. In those days so long ago, you intended to harm me, but God intended it for good, to accomplish the saving of many lives. So do not fear, my dear brothers. I will care for you and your children and your children's children, and together, as a family numerous as the stars, may we seek to be God's blessing to all generations."

Israel's twelve sons lived together in peace and

harmony from that day on. Eleven returned to Goshen, to tend their flocks and to train their children in the way of the Lord. Joseph went back to Pharaoh's palace. There he remained, the king's most trusted advisor, until the days of his old age. His sons Ephraim and Manasseh grew to manhood and had children of their own, children who knew and honored the God of Abraham, Isaac, Israel and their grandfather Joseph.

When he was near death, Joseph called the huge clan to his bedside. "Soon I will die," he told them. "But know for a certainty that God will keep the promise He made to our fathers. He will surely come and get you, and bring you back to Canaan, the land of promise. Walk in His ways, that you might be found faithful when that great day comes."

Then, like his father Israel before him, Joseph made his family promise that when they returned to Canaan, they would take his body with them and bury it there. So at last, Joseph—the daydreamer, the slave, the prime minister of Egypt, and finally the head of a great family— went to be with the Lord when he was 110 years old.

His descendants continued to live in the land of

Egypt for many generations. There they grew strong and became a learned people, mastering many valuable skills. And then at long last, the Lord kept the promise He had made so many years earlier. He brought them out of Egypt and back to the Promised Land. By this time, Joseph's family had grown to such large numbers, the people organized themselves into twelve tribes, one for each of Israel's twelve sons. It was to these twelve tribes that God gave His commandments and His Holy Scripture. It was through the sons and daughters of Israel that people everywhere learned about righteousness. As numerous as the stars in the night sky, Israel's family continues to this very day, God's blessing to all generations.